For His Name
Yeshua
ישרע

Rebecca Hazelton

OlivePress
צהר זית
Messianic & Christian Publisher

City of David excavation site.

Yeshua

ישרע

YHVH is my:
Salvation
Deliverer
Helper
Healer
Rescuer

שם (shem) = name
a mark of individuality,
honor, authority, character

Restoring the Name and Reputation of the Jewish Messiah

For His Name YESHUA ישוע

Restoring the Name and Reputation of the Jewish Messiah

ISBN 978-1-941173-01-5

Copyright © 2014 by Rebecca Hazelton

Published by
Olive Press Messianic and Christian Publisher
olivepresspublisher.com

Messianic & Christian Publisher

Printed in the USA.

1. Hebrew Roots Study 2. Spiritual Growth 3. Jewish Topic Study

All photos © 2014 by Rebecca Hazelton.
(The front cover photo is from the Biblical Tamar Park in Israel.)
(The back cover photo is from the Citiy of David excavation site.)

Though he was in the form of God,
he did not regard equality with God
something to be possessed by force.
On the contrary, he emptied himself,
in that he took the form of a slave by
becoming like human beings are. And
when he appeared as a human being,
he humbled himself still more
by becoming obedient even to death —
death on a stake as a criminal!
Therefore God raised him to the
highest place and gave him the
Name above every name;
that in honor of the name given Yeshua,
every knee will bow — in heaven,
on earth and under the earth — and
every tongue will acknowledge that
Yeshua the Messiah is ADONAI —
to the glory of God the Father.

Philippians 2:6-11

Dedicated to:

Yeshua, without You, I am nothing. Thank You for Your forgiveness, mercy, and grace. I love You and can't wait to be with You face to face for eternity!

Millie, Millie, Millie – Thank you for being the most authentic role model of what it means to be like Yeshua. We have had such sweet moments of fellowship. May we come to know Him better still!

All our Jewish Mishpacha (family) - Maybe now you will know why we love you so much. Someone loves you even more and is waiting for an opportunity to reveal Himself to you.

Table of Contents

Preface

The concept of this book emerged from a passion for Yeshua and His Hebrew name. As I saw His name in the Hebrew Scriptures, I was stirred to think about how His name had been lost in the course of time and the translation of the Scriptures into other languages and cultures. My original idea was to have a simple booklet, sharing the Scriptures that showed the word "Salvation" in the Hebrew Tanach (Old Testament) and sharing my passion for His name in an exhortation to various groups to rediscover His Hebrew given name and restore it to common usage.

I was encouraged by Messianic Jewish Publishers to develop my booklet into a book. After much prayer and fasting, I began to write what was on my heart and it flowed into what you have in your hands now. The Father gave me the idea for the concept of excavating and how that connects with digging deeper into our history and the foundations of our religions to discover the Truth of His Word and our Faith. My dear friend Cheryl Zehr helped me put the finishing touches on it and in her graciousness agreed to publish it for me, when Messianic Jewish Publishers could not fit it in after all. Thank you Cheryl!

Tom and Mary,
May YHVH continue
to lead you in paths
of righteousness for His
name's sake.
Blessings!
Rebecca

8

As I call upon His Name to *"show me great and mighty things which I do not know"* (Jeremiah 33:3), He is revealing layers and layers of the depths of the riches and treasures hidden in His Word. This is an ongoing process. I have not arrived. Therefore, as you read this book, remember that I am mere "flesh" and that I don't have the complete picture yet. I look through a glass dimly. As I grow and develop a deeper relationship to my Savior, Yeshua, submitting my mind, will, emotions, and entire being to Him daily, He will continue to guide me on the course of my life to correct, align, position, and purpose me according to His will for me. A year from now I may wish I had said things differently, or have a deeper understanding of what He is trying to show me. So, I offer, in its incomplete form, my passion for Him and His Name. I will only encourage you to dig and discover for yourself if what I have shared is the Truth and deserves attention.

I do know that He will complete the work He has begun in me until the Day He returns and restores all things and corrects all our (mis)understandings. What a Day that will be! Until then......

For His Name,
Rebecca Hazelton

Begun in a camp in the woods of Maine in the summer of 2011, continued on a farmette in Virginia during the Spring of 2013, and finished in Israel during Chanukah 2013.

Exit from Hezekiah's tunnel.
In this book, we are going on an exciting, spiritual excavation.
Come join me!

1

An Introduction Along the Way

**Trust in the LORD with all your heart; do not
depend on your own understanding. Seek his will in
all you do, and he will show you which path to take.**
(Proverbs 3:5,6 NLT)

Our first visit to Israel was in the summer/fall of 2002.
This was during what was known as the "Second Intifada"
where buses were being blown up and tourists were few and far
between. The Lord had told us to go without any reservations
to see what *He* could do. We were to learn His people and
their ways. I had spent a number of years overseas and was
familiar with traveling to a foreign country. Starting with my
first overseas trip to Northern Ireland during the "troubles" in
1978, I have had no fear of going into a potentially dangerous
situation, because security is not found in the absence of
danger, but in the presence of Yeshua. I am at rest as long as I
know I am under His command and in the center of His will.

This was a new experience, however, for my husband,
Ronald, who had only traveled in the United States. Upon
arrival at Ben Gurion airport, the whirlwind began as we were
ushered into a "shirut" (taxi van) going to Jerusalem. All the
men sat in the front and were jabbering away in Hebrew. The
women sat in the back. I was sitting beside a young English
speaking woman and she was asking where we were going to
stay in Jerusalem. I told her we did not know. I said we had
heard of several places, but we did not have any reservations.
She suggested we check out the Finnish Mission on Shivtei

11

Yisrael Street. She said it was a nice guest house. We had heard of the Finnish Mission and we had a map of Jerusalem. We took this as a sign and asked the driver to drop us off at the Jaffa Gate. There we were, a middle aged couple with two backpacks, being dropped off in the middle of Jerusalem.

The hustle and bustle of Friday afternoon was apparent as we began to make our way toward the street that had been recommended to us. Thankfully, it was not far. As we encountered people along the way we began to inquire if they knew where the Finnish Mission was located. No one spoke English and the realities of being in a foreign land were becoming apparent. Travel is always tiring and now we were in 90+ degree (Fareinheit) weather with heavy backpacks on our backs. We were hoping to get an answer soon.

One of the men we asked turned around after a few steps and said, "Light hair—right there." We thought about Finnish people being from Scandinavia and most having light hair, so we took this as a direction to check out the place where he was pointing. It was a compound with high iron gates. We looked inside and all we saw were Asian people!

Thinking we might be lost, we cautiously ventured through the gate door and found an entrance to the front building. On the mailbox were the letters FELM. Ah. Perhaps we have found the right place. We rang the doorbell and in a few minutes the massive door swung open and an elderly Jamaican woman greeted us with, "Praise the Lord. Someone is here!"

This was our introduction to Phinette, an 82-year-old woman who had been praying for two months for people to come fill this guest house. We asked her if there was a place we might be able to stay and she directed us, finally, to the real Finnish people in charge. They quickly gave us accommodations and we settled in for the Sabbath which was announced by sirens. We were so thankful for a place to lay our heads.

Our adventure was about to begin.

During those troubled times, not only were tourists scarce, but also volunteers. When we inquired about helping out at the compound, we were told that they had never had volunteers from anywhere but Finland, and we had not gone through the normal approval process. However, they were willing to try us out for a week to see how things would go.

To make a long and beautiful story short, within a week, we ended up receiving room and board and holding the keys to the entire compound. We were entrusted with locking up at night and caring for any weekend guests that might arrive. I worked with the cleaning staff and Ronald worked with the maintenance man. Our six hour work day included meals and devotions and we kept being told not to work so hard! They were so thankful for Ronald's willingness to climb the rafters to clean out gutters and cut off dead palm tree branches because everyone else was afraid of heights! By the time we left, the guest house was full. Phinette's prayers had been answered.

In the meantime, I began the tedious job of learning Hebrew. We were introduced to a Messianic Hebrew congregation who seemed to really enjoy my violin. It was a pleasure. During that first eight week stay in Israel, the Lord began to do a deep work in my spirit. Our first visit to the "Kotel" (Wailing Wall) in the Old City was overwhelming. Ronald had gone into the men's prayer area and I stood behind the dividing wall. Immediately I felt an overwhelming cry come from deep within my being. Tears began to flow freely and the words, "open their eyes," came from my lips. I would come to understand later that when I was praying that prayer, the Lord was ready to open *my* eyes to truths I had never been able to see before. I fell in love with the Jewish people and I would come to fall even more in love with my Savior as I began to learn His Jewish, Biblical heritage.

What I am going to share in this book comes from that well spring of longing for both Jews and Christians to have

13

their "eyes opened." I believe something is missing that has caused a void in our understanding of the God of Abraham, Isaac, and Jacob. I want to reveal the passion of my heart, in the hopes that it will ignite a fire of desire to really come to know Yeshua, the Savior of both Jews and Gentiles.

While writing my passion, however, I asked myself this question many times: Why do we need another book? The only answer I can give is that I feel the Lord is requiring it of me, therefore it is a *mitzvah* (commandment) from Him and I desire to please my Father. However, I do agree with King Shlomo (Solomon) when he said:

> **And furthermore, my son, be admonished: of making many books there is no end; and much study is a weariness of the flesh. The end of the matter, all having been heard: fear God, and keep His commandments; for this is the whole man. For God shall bring every work into the judgment concerning every hidden thing, whether it be good or whether it be evil. (Ecclesiastes 12:12-14 JPS)**

I have been a simple believer in the God of Israel since I was 5 years old and only wanted to serve Him. I had a brief period in mid-life when I doubted, rebelled, and even went through a shockingly unexpected divorce. However, those experiences helped me reexamine my faith and the faith of my fathers. In repentance and returning, I felt the "cloak of religion" fall off my shoulders and a real relationship with God begin to deepen and develop. I have a call to exhort and encourage brethren from both sides of the Judeo-Christian persuasion to rethink, reexamine, and dig for a deeper truth which will unlock the door to an amazing relationship with a living God through the promised Messiah of Israel, Yeshua ben David.

In recent years, my husband and I have gone through the fires of persecution. We lost almost every material thing when we developed a subdivision on land Ronald owns in Maine. Ronald, with his flaming red hair and ruddy complexion may just look like his ancestor, King David to whom God gave very specific instructions for building the Temple. In the same way, Ronald received the pattern for developing the land and what to name it: "God's Acres." This was not done presumptuously. It was done out of obedience and reverence to God and to His Name.

We presented this name in the final approval meeting with the Planning Board of the Town, and declared that it was the land of the God of Abraham, Isaac, and Jacob. In southern USA that would be acceptable, but in New England it is looked upon as a "religious" name and shunned. Every sign we ever erected with the name "God's Acres" on it was torn down or stolen. The last permanent permitted sign was even sawed down by a chain saw! The road name "Zion Way" seemed to also evoke hateful reactions and the road sign was also regularly removed. We have been hated by un-peaceful neighbors who wanted to take everything we owned to get rid of us. In that respect, we can identify, in a very tiny degree, with what Israel faces every day with her neighbors and their desire for the Jewish people to be "driven into the sea."

Initially, we saw the subdivision as our provision for returning to Israel more permanently, but now we see it as our "crucible." There was much we needed to go through in order to have a deeper understanding and connection to God's people and to deepen our own relationship with Him. We ended up losing the 22 lots of the subdivision in a foreclosure, which is another whole story! However, we are rich in faith and trust and full of hope. Our Father is a great and mighty God and we thank Him every day for every little thing we can think of.

When I look back on all the amazing divine appointments and provisions of our life "Along the Way," I am filled with

15

praise and thanksgiving. We have not had a home for several years now, but we have never missed a meal unless we were fasting and we have never slept on the street. We have always had a bed, even if it was on a floor. We have stayed in camps in the woods without running water or electricity, slept in a church, and stayed in beautiful houses. We would be amiss if we didn't mention and thank the many people who have opened up their homes to us. Our "Helping Hands" ministry may have been the reason, but you trusted us and took us in. Thank you. It would take a whole book to tell the many, many stories of all the beautiful lives that have touched us and hopefully we have been a blessing in return! We love you all!

Because I come from a "Christian" background, my heart bleeds for what has been done to the Jewish people at the hands of those who call themselves Christians and in the name of Jesus Christ.

Therefore, I would like to begin by saying something important to the Jewish people.

I come humbly before you to ask forgiveness for the errors of my ancestors. Those who have represented "Jesus" as a Gentile, making Him the "head" of a religion, have missed the mark and misunderstood G-d's plan for Israel and the nations. His name has been defiled among the nations just as G-d's personal Name has been defiled and misrepresented. When I use the tetragramation YHVH[1], with the English letters, to indicate the personal Name of the G-d of Avraham, Yitzach, and Y'akov, I mean no disrespect to the Sacred Name. I am not indicating a pronunciation or usage of the Name in a "flippant manner." If I am speaking His Name – I generally use "HaShem" or "Adonai," as when reciting Scriptures.

There is no excuse for the atrocities that have been perpetrated through the "Christian" church and in the name of "Jesus Christ" against the Jewish people. When our ancestors forced conversion upon your people and forced you to forsake your Hebrew heritage and roots, it was a travesty beyond imagination! All of the persecution, pogroms, and finally the Holocaust are deep scars on the souls of your people. I grieve for your loss. When our forefathers changed Yeshua's Name to a Greek form (Jesus), they took away the meaning of His Name and deprived you of your Messiah!

My purpose in this book is to inspire an awakening in your spirit to the truths embedded in your Holy Scriptures. Only the Spirit of YHVH can reveal truth, and my prayer is that you will discover that Yeshua, from the tribe of Judah and the House of David, is in fact the promised Messiah. I am asking that you look into the claim of Yeshua being the Messiah, by having the courage to ask G-d to open your spiritual eyes as you read the Scriptures. I have included references from the TaNaKH² which reveal the Name of Yeshua embedded in the verses and also references which are prophesies fulfilled by Yeshua in the B'rit Hadashah writings (New Covenant). Thank you for preserving the writings of the Covenant Scriptures through the centuries and being the bearer of the truth of the Word of G-d and the bearer of the Messiah through the lineage of Judah and the house of David to which we could come to faith in Him whose eminent return will restore the Kingdom of G-d to earth and correct all our misrepresentations and misunderstandings! Hallelujah. May it be in our day!

Now a word to my Christian readers. To be a lover of Yeshua is to be a lover of His people. You can't have one without the other. In chapter 10 (p. 105), you will find a prayer for Christians who want to come into alignment with the plan of YHVH and the move of His Spirit in this time.

Ok. Let's all begin a spiritual archeological excavating and rebuilding venture to uncover and restore deep Truth about the Name of the Jewish Messiah, Yeshua. The Scriptures at the beginning of each chapter are tools that we need for this project, so don't skip over them!

I've got my shovel ready to dig in. Will you join me?

----

[1] I use YHVH for the Hebrew יהוה (Yud Hey Vav Hey) known as the "tetragrammation" which is the personal Name of Elohim (God) – see Exodus 3:13-15. His Name is indeed sacred and Adonai or HaShem is commonly used to honor the 2nd (3rd in the Hebrew Bible) *"mitzvah"* (commandment) to "not take the name of YHVH lightly (in vain). I am not indicating a pronunciation of these four letters. I am simply acknowledging that our Elohim (God) has a personal Name that I want to honor. I believe it has been "lost" in the mainstream of Christian and even Jewish Scriptures and literature. I mean no disrespect to Jewish people by using the four letters to represent HaShem in this book.

I capitalize pronouns, such as "Him," "His," etc, when referring to Yeshua or YHVH to honor and respect His position of authority and sovereignty.

[2] TaNaKH is an acronym formed from the initial Hebrew letters of the Masoretic Text's three traditional subdivisions: The **Torah** ("Teaching," also known as the Five Books of Moses), **Nevi'im** ("Prophets") and **Ketuvim** ("Writings")—hence **TaNaKh**.

As much as possible, I interpose the Hebrew transliterated names and titles with the common English version. If I use the English, the Hebrew transliteration will be in ( ). If I use a Hebrew transliteration, the common English word will be in ( ).

2

Excavating Before Rebuilding

As some people were remarking about the Temple, how beautiful its stone work and memorial decorations were, he said, "The time is coming when what you see here will be totally destroyed—not a single stone will be left standing!" (Luke 21:5-6)

"Why do you call me 'Lord! Lord!' but not do what I say? Everyone who comes to me, hears my words and acts on them—I will show you what he is like; he is like someone building a house who <u>dug deep and laid the foundation on bedrock</u>. When a flood came, the torrent beat against that house but couldn't shake it, because it was constructed well. And whoever hears my words but doesn't act on them is like someone who built his house on the ground without any foundation. As soon as the river struck it, it collapsed and that house became a horrendous wreck!" (Luke 6:46-49)

For we are God's co-workers; you are God's field, God's building. Using the grace God gave me, I laid a foundation, like a skilled master-builder; and another man is building on it. But let each one be careful how he builds. For no one can lay any foundation other than the one already laid, which is Yeshua the Messiah. Some will use gold, silver or precious stones in building on this foundation; while others will use wood, grass or straw. But each one's work will be shown for what it is; the Day will disclose it, because it will be revealed by fire—the fire will test the quality of each one's work. If the work someone has built on the foundation survives, he will receive a reward; if it is burned up, he will have to bear the loss: he will still escape with his life, but it will be like escaping through a fire. Don't you know that you people are God's temple and that God's Spirit lives in you? (I Corinthians 3:9-16)

During our fourth visit to Israel in 2010, we stayed in the Old City for most of the three months we were there. I had fun with my violin, playing on the streets for "pennies from heaven." Our friend James was already doing this regularly with his guitar and he invited me to join him one balmy evening in the Mamila shopping mall outside the "Old City" walls. Children would come and drop coins in our cases and sometimes would dance around the courtyard area where we played.

One time as I was walking through that outdoor mall, I noticed many of the buildings had stones with numbers on them. I came to understand that they were buildings that had been carefully torn down, their stones numbered, and then rebuilt once the excavation and preparation for the site was completed. Of course any excavation in Israel involves archeology. There are millennia of history, mysteries, and truths of the past to uncover. Many of the buildings needed to be rebuilt because their foundations would have been unstable from the many earthquakes that have rocked Jerusalem over the centuries.

I believe we must excavate the building site of our religions. The building is not standing very straight and it looks like it is about to crumble. Some of its walls have already fallen from the shaking that has taken place. Something must be wrong with the foundation. We need to remove the structure above ground and dig into the foundation to see, first of all, what is wrong, and then make it right! Finally, we can rebuild the ruins and repair the broken walls. The house will be much stronger and will stand, if we do it right. We're not going to bring in a wrecking ball because we might smash stones that need to be reset. They may have beauty and potential. We must be careful to do this right. But it must be done, otherwise the house will become a ruin.

I am not a scholar, but I love the Scriptures.[1] I am not an archeologist, but I love to dig into the Word, research word origins, and question to find original meanings and sources. I do not simply accept what I've always been taught nor what others say.

My desire is that in doing this "excavation," you will hear with spiritual ears, and see with spiritual eyes, the longing of your Father, calling for you to dig, search, uncover, come back, return, restore, rebuild, and fall in love with Him again— or for the first time. As we see Yeshua in the Scriptures and do spiritual archeology, we will begin to see the foundation stones of our religions exposed. We will be amazed and blessed to find that there is indeed a "pearl of great price" and we will hopefully be willing to sell all that we have (and are) to gain that pearl.

Our zeal for the "Lord of Hosts" will become the driving force to see others restored to their Messiah or be introduced to the Savior of the World. Life will come out of dead stones, which will shout in praise to YHVH, the Eternal God of Avraham (Abraham), Yitzchak (Isaac), and Y'akov (Jacob). We will look to the fulfillment of the Scriptures to see our Messiah return to claim His rightful place as King of Kings and Lord of Lords to the Glory of YHVH! We will be prepared to be the Bride of Messiah, ready in white garments to meet our Bridegroom, Yeshua. Our love and excitement will grow until we **all** cry out "Baruch Haba B'Shem Adonai" ("Blessed is He who comes in the Name of the Lord").

This is an exploration. We are going to be archeologists for truth. We are going to carefully tear down—numbering and preserving each piece, then dig till we find the true foundation and rebuild on it.

Are you ready? Put on your gear, grab your equipment, and let's go.

----

[1] I did attend seminary in Virginia in 1989 but that doesn't make me a scholar. I am much more of a "heart" person than a "head" person, but I appreciate the research others have done to enhance my study. I hope I have given due credit, where credit is due.

3

Religion vs Relationship

You will Rebuild the ancient ruins,

Raise foundations from ages past,

and be called "Repairer of broken walls,

Restorer of streets to live in." (Isaiah 58:12)

The first thing we need to carefully dismantle is our "religion." While participating in a prison ministry in Alabama several years ago, I met an amazing Jewish woman who was "doing her time." In the midst of her confinement, she had met her Messiah and become a believer in Yeshua. We developed a deep friendship. During our visit, she shared a quote by a friend of hers whose name I only know as "Daniel."

Religion is man's misunderstanding of God,
for God has no misunderstanding of man,
and if man understood God,
there would be no religion,
there would only be relationship.

There is a profound truth in these words and I share them frequently. From the beginning of time in Genesis (B'resheet) chapter 1 verse 1, YHVH has desired a relationship with His creation. Everything in the Hebrew TaNaKH (Old Testament) through to the end of the New Covenant (B'rit Hadashah)[1] speaks of this.

Beginning in Genesis 1 we see YHVH speaking order into chaos. We see Him setting up a Plan that yields the peaceful fruit of righteousness (right order). The verse heading this chapter from Isaiah 58 comes toward the end of his prophesy to Israel and Judah as he begins to speak of a restoration of both a physical and a spiritual Israel. This section is full of exhortation and promises. YHVH is challenging Israel to consider what she has been doing out of performance of duty and not from the Spirit of Elohim. YHVH is exposing the "religious spirit" of the day and declaring what He truly desires from her. He is begging for a relationship with them, not religious duty.

I believe YHVH is saying the same things to us today. "Religion" has become so engrained in our way of thinking and culture that we are also "performing" out of duty, having no idea where all our traditions have come from. We've built a house, but the foundation stones are so obscured we don't even know what they are anymore. We believe the house is beautiful and ornate, but it is actually a "religious" façade. Both Judaism and Christianity have become religions unto themselves and in opposition to each other. Relationship with YHVH has become ritualized, institutionalized, and dead. There is no life in most of our churches and synagogues and we wonder why we even attend them. Some have become the local "club house" where all types of social activity is available, but no one seeks YHVH and the power of His Spirit has left without anyone really noticing.

What has often prevented Jewish people from re-considering Yeshua as Messiah has been religion. Jewish people, being the astute people they are, see a double standard and lack of authenticity in "Christians," giving them no reason to even consider the claims of Yeshua as Messiah. YHVH's original Plan was to be a conversion of heart, not conversion to another religion, as we will discover later in our excavating.

One time, while I was in Israel, I read a book of quotes by Jewish writers. Here is one passage I think is especially appropriate for today:

"Religion has become a substitute for the couch of the psychoanalyst. It is expected to give us peace of mind, to bring us happiness, to guarantee us good health; and to assure us of never ending prosperity. This religion is not God oriented, but man centered. Man is not required to serve God, but God is meant to serve man. It is the typical religion of the middle class. We have everything now: jobs, professions, homes, cars, insurance policies; and we also have a God. ... One can never tell when one may need Him. Our religion is a prop for our prosperity and comforts. No one is concerned with the Word of God. No one listens. No one obeys. The function of our "awakened" piety is to confirm us in our habits and customary ways of thought. We believe in God, but we also limit His authority. We prescribe for Him how to act toward us. Truth for Him is what we hold to be true, Right, what we consider right. He can ask of us no more than what we ask of ourselves. Most important of all, He is to be considerate. In no way may He inconvenience us or interfere with our comforts and pleasures." [2]

I'd like to have the veil removed from my eyes so that the Master Builder is able to reveal to me how He sees things. Then I can see more clearly how to repair the foundation of my faith. I don't want religion. I want relationship! How about you?

----
[1] The term "New Covenant" (B'rit – Covenant; Hadasha – New) is taken from the passage in Jeremiah 31:30-33 (31-34 in most Bibles) where it says *"Here, the days are coming,"* says ADONAI, *"when I will make a new covenant with the house of Isra'el and with the house of Y'hudah..... For this is the covenant I will make with the house of Isra'el after those*

days," says ADONAI: "I will put my Torah within them and write it on their hearts; I will be their God, and they will be my people." Also, when Yeshua declares during the Passover Seder before His death *"This cup is the New Covenant, ratified by my blood, which is being poured out for you."* The Hebrew word "khadash" (Strongs 2318/19) means new, but also implies to "renew" or "repair" (not replace). So, understanding this, when you see the word "new" as in "New Covenant" or "One New Man" – remember that it is not as if there is anything "new under the sun" or that the former covenants that YHVH made are no longer valid, but that YHVH's plan is always "renewing and repairing His relationship with us." He makes us "new" – renewing our relationship with/to Him, renewing our minds, etc. We see this in the phrase "new moon" (the same root word used for month). The moon is actually not "new" because it is the same moon as the month before, it is just "renewing" itself. It is fresh, revived. Keep this concept in mind as you read this book.

[2] Eliezer Berkovits, quoted in the book, *Returning: Exercises in Repentance,* edited by Jonathan Magonet, published by The Reform Synagogues of Great Britain, London, 1975; re-published by the Bloch Publishing Company (the oldest Jewish Publishing Company in the U.S.), 1997. (I read the book in 2003 at a library in the Galilee.)

4.

Sound the Shofar! Remove the Veil!

On this mountain he will destroy the veil which covers the face of <u>all peoples</u>, the veil enshrouding <u>all</u> the nations. (Isaiah 25:7)

For I do not desire, brethren, that you should be ignorant of this mystery, lest you should be wise in your own opinion, that <u>blindness in part</u> has happened to Israel until the fullness of the Gentiles has come in. (Romans 11:25 NKJV)

What is more, their minds were made stonelike; for to this day the same veil remains over them when they read the Old Covenant; it has not been unveiled, because only by the Messiah is the veil taken away. Yes, till today, whenever Moshe is read, a veil lies over their heart. "But," says the Torah, "whenever someone turns to ADONAI, the veil is taken away." Now, "ADONAI" in this text means the Spirit. And where the Spirit of ADONAI is, there is freedom. So all of us, with faces unveiled, see as in a mirror the glory of the Lord; and we are being changed into his very image, from one degree of glory to the next, by ADONAI the Spirit..... So if indeed our Good News is veiled, it is veiled only to those in the process of being lost. They do not come to trust because the god of the 'olam hazeh has blinded

27

**their minds, in order to prevent them from seeing
the light shining from the Good News about the
glory of the Messiah, who is the image of God.
(II Corinthians 3:14-18; 4:3-4)**

Every time Ronald and I have been called to go to Israel,
it seems to be the will of YHVH that we do not know where
we are going to end up or what we are going to be doing there.
Sometimes I have fretted over the uncertainties, but the Father
has been faithful to set up our agenda to such a degree that in
the end, I am humbled and marvel at His goodness! Our fourth
trip in 2010 was no exception.

We were given very little notice to go. We were to
be there during the Fall Feasts of YHVH. We had specific
instructions to be in Jerusalem for Rosh Hashana (The Feast
of Trumpets). We were picked up at the airport by our dear
Jewish friends from Bat Yam and warmly welcomed into their
home. They wanted us to stay for the holidays, but we said we
needed to be in Jerusalem for the Feast. They asked if we had
a place to go and we said no.

We had a list of potential places, but had had no time
to call and make arrangements. Time was running out. Rosh
Hashana was fast approaching. I prayed and asked the Lord to
be gracious to us and please let the first call be an open door.
I took the list and pointed to a name and number and made
the call. The miraculous answer was yes and we were off to
Jerusalem the next day.

We stayed with this amazing couple the first week and
celebrated the New Year (Rosh Hashana) with them. That was
all the time they could give us, so we moved to a place in the
Jewish quarter of the Old City the next week in preparation for
Yom Kippur (Day of Atonement). We were in the Ten Days of
Awe (the ten days between Rosh Hashana and Yom Kippur).
Unlike our first visits in 2002 and 2003, Jerusalem was bursting

with tourists and pilgrims for the feasts. We were blessed to even find a "room in the inn"! During those nights in the Old City we were housed in a basement-type room with a small window near the very high ceiling. The window acted like a funnel for the sound of the street above it.

We soon discovered that tours of the Old City were being given all night long during that holiday time. We were right under a stopping point along the tour, where a major battle to keep the Old City had ensued, in part of the 1948 War of Independence. About 40 people had died and were temporarily buried there until after the victory of the Six Day War in 1967. During the whole night we heard loud speakers in Hebrew and people talking. It sounded as if they were in the room with us! It was assaulting to the flesh, but our spirits were stirred that there was something deeper going on. Ronald was prompted to get up at 2 o'clock one night and was told to go to the "Wall" (Kotel). He began to make his way there and found that he could not even get to the courtyard leading to the Wall. The people there were packed like sardines from the Wall to the top of the stairs. He eventually made his way down and to the Wall itself, but it took a very long time. He was overwhelmed with this experience. Here, in the middle of the night, there were so many people in Jerusalem, that you couldn't move an inch?! What was happening?

The following day I was conversing with an Orthodox Rabbi's wife who was a neighbor of where we were staying. She was all upset about the disturbances in the night. She said I should write to the mayor of Jerusalem to voice my complaint that such things should not be allowed to go on! I listened to her rant and then graciously made my leave. Her husband and another Rabbi were outside their apartment. They were expressing their amazement at how God was moving among the people and fulfilling the prophesies of the Scriptures. They were saying, "They have heard the sound of the Shofar. They

don't even know why they are here, but they have heard it!"
These were Ultra Orthodox Jewish rabbis who understood
what YHVH's plan was. I was again humbled and amazed.
Two different people. Two different perspectives. One
from the flesh. One from the Spirit. "They heard the sound of
the Shofar." These Rabbis knew that for most it was not the
physical sound that they had heard. They heard a call from
YHVH Himself! The Shofar (an ancient instrument made
from a ram's horn) is known as "the voice of YHVH." When
you hear its voice by an anointed sounder, you should feel the
heavens break open. For too long the sound of the Shofar has
either been missing from Christian churches or has not been
sounded with its intended purpose.

There are two veils indicated in Scriptures quoted at the
beginning of this chapter.[1] The first veil is the one over all the
nations. The Hebrew of this verse literally says the "face of
the covering" over the nations. It is like the concept of an
envelope. Something is covering up the contents. The second
veil is a specific one for the chosen people of Israel and is more
like blindness. Their veil has had a purpose of allowing the
Gentiles to become believers in Yeshua as it indicates in the
Romans 11 and II Corinthians verses quoted. It will be removed
when the fullness of the Gentiles has "come in." What does
this mean? It means that the "age of the Gentiles" is going to
come to a close and the shift and focus will turn back to the
Jewish people. It also means that there will come a day when
the veil is completely removed and all Israel will see clearly,
have their eyes open, and their Messiah Yeshua will reveal
Himself to them like Joseph revealed himself to his brothers
in Genesis 45.
I also believe that this "time of the Gentiles" has been a
test for the Gentiles. YHVH wants to see what is in our hearts in
the same way Israel was tested in the wilderness. (Deuteronomy

8:2-5) What do we do with and how do we treat the people of YHVH? Do we spurn and discard them? Or do we love and bless them? Are we worthy to be called "sheep" because we *"did it to the least of these, my brethren"*? (Matthew 25:40) Let us look at a very strategic Scripture which I believe is a prophecy for our times. It appears in two different prophets' books. When YHVH repeats something more than once, it usually means we need to pay attention!

But in the acharit-ha yamim [latter days] it will come about that the mountain of ADONAI's house will be established as the most important mountain. It will be regarded more highly than the other hills and peoples will stream there. Many Gentiles will go and say, "Come, let's go up to the mountain of ADONAI, to the house of the God of Ya'akov (Jacob)! He will teach us about His ways, and we will walk in His paths." For out of Tziyon will go forth Torah, the word of ADONAI from Yerushalayim. (Micah 4:1-2 and Isaiah 2:3-4)

In the Scriptures we always see that when YHVH is about to perform a major shift in history, things are foreshadowed as a preparation. What we have seen in the past 65+ years is the reemergence of the Nation of Israel and the return of His people to the land as never before in history. So many Scriptures are being fulfilled![2] It would seem as if the Spirit is saying that in the latter days there will come a turning of direction back to Zion, back to the place where YHVH chose to place His name—Jerusalem.[3] The move of the Spirit in these days is back to the root, back to the origins—back to relationship with our Creator as it was intended to be in the Garden. The Gospel has gone out to the "ends of the earth" and now it is returning to the source, back to Zion—the spiritual Jerusalem. The restoration of all things is what the Messiah is doing. He is beginning it now. Will we "stream" into the flow of His Spirit? Will we align ourselves and focus our attention back to the God of Israel?Will we allow Him to teach us of His ways, His Torah (instruction), and His purposes?

When Yeshua came the first time He ushered in the New Covenant prophesied in Jeremiah 31:31-34. His people were given the opportunity to come into alignment with the Plan of YHVH. They were invited to join Messiah and enter into newness of life. Some "left all" and did so. These Jewish believers followed what was called "The Way." They are our forefathers of the faith. They did not begin a new religion. They understood what it meant to be "born again" by the Spirit and enter into relationship with YHVH through acceptance of Yeshua as Messiah. It was what Yeshua was all about. The blood atonement and sacrifice were made so that we could come back to the Father in a reconciliation of relationship producing righteousness. There were others who did not join the move of the Spirit but chose to remain in their man made religion and traditions and as they say "the rest is history." YHVH did not abandon those who stayed behind, but they missed *"the time of your visitation"* (Luke 19:44).

The Holy Spirit is giving us the same choice today. It is time for the Lion of the tribe of Judah to return in power to rule the nations. Will we join in the move of the Spirit and align ourselves with the Plan of YHVH? Are we willing to look at and possibly forsake our religious traditions for a deeper relationship with our Savior? Are we willing to humble ourselves before His people, the Jewish people, to love and restore the name and reputation of their Messiah?

I believe the veil that covers the nations begins to be re-moved when the Shofar is heard. May we all hear the sound of the Shofar, the voice of YHVH, so that the veil will be lifted from our eyes. We see an awakening among Jewish people to their Messiah Yeshua. The veil is being lifted from their eyes now. The time of the Gentiles is coming to a rapid close. The Messianic Age is about to be ushered in. Hallelujah! Blow the Shofar! Here is my prayer for all of us:

"Glorious Father, Yeshua HaMashiach, and Ruach HaKodesh, please give us, Your beloved ones, the power to think, act, and feel with great wisdom, as You disclose truth, and instruction concerning things before unknown. Give us correct and precise knowledge of You. Bring the Light of Yeshua into our souls so that we will perceive, discover, and discern that You have invited us to a feast! May we indeed understand the amazing wealth You have promised us in our inheritance, and abundance in every area of our being. May we know Your exceeding power to perform miracles and bring excellence to our souls as we trust totally in You.

May we know that this power is a working power that has the same strength and force that worked to raise You, Yeshua Messiah, from the dead and appointed and conferred upon You a Kingdom at the right hand of the Father in Heaven. This position is far above each and every ruler, prince of demons, authority, power, dominion, or any other name that can be named either in this age or in the age to come. You have subjected all things under Your feet and have been bestowed upon the position of supreme Lord and husband over all the called out ones, which is Your family. May we be filled completely with the presence, power, and riches of You, who fills all in all!" (My amplified paraphrase of the Ephesians 1:17-23 prayer after doing a thorough word study of every word in this passage.)

33

----

[1] Verses referred to in this paragraph: Romans 11:25-26; Isaiah 25:7; Deuteronomy 8:2; Matthew 25:31-46

[2] Here is a list of Scripture references you can look up on your own. It is just a partial list, but it will give you a taste of the amazing things being fulfilled in our time and before our very eyes! Isaiah 2:3,3; 14:1; 43:6; 44:26; 49:14-23; 51:1-3; 61:4,5; 62:1-7; Jeremiah 31:8-11; 50:4-6; Ezekiel 34:11-16; 36, 37; Hosea 11:10; Amos 9:9-15; Micah 4:1-2, 6; Zechariah 14:16

[3] Psalm 132:13-18

5

What is in a Name?

שׁם (shem) = name
(a mark of individuality, honor,
authority, character)

"Don't be afraid, Miriam, for you have found favor with God. Look! You will become pregnant, you will give birth to a son, and you are to name him Yeshua. He will be great, he will be called Son of Ha'Elyon. ADONAI, God, will give him the throne of his forefather David and he will rule the House of Ya'akov forever—there will be no end to his Kingdom." "How can this be," asked Miryam of the angel, "since I am a virgin?" The angel answered her, 'The Ruach HaKodesh will come over you, the power of Ha'Elyon will cover you. Therefore the holy child born to you will be called the Son of God."

(Luke 1:30-35)

"She will give birth to a son, and you are to name him Yeshua, which means 'ADONAI saves' because he will save His people from their sins."

(Matthew 1:21)

On the eighth day, when it was time for his *b'rit-milah*, he was given the name Yeshua, which is what the angel had called him before his conception.

(Luke 2:21)

35

In today's Western society, the naming of a child is generally arbitrary. Parents might like the sound of a particular name, or they name a child after a person they know. In the Catholic tradition, children are often named after "saints." Rarely do we name a child for the meaning of the name or the purpose or destiny of the child. *"In Jewish thought, a name is not merely an arbitrary designation, a random combination of sounds. The name conveys the nature and essence of the thing named. It represents the history and reputation of the being named."*[1]

In the Jewish culture, a name assigns a person a position. It is interesting that a Jewish male child is generally not named until their B'rit Milah (circumcision) eight days after birth. It gives the parents time to decide what destiny this child might have or what character qualities are already displayed in the first days of life.[2] When YHVH designates a name for the child, as in the case of Yeshua, He is already declaring His purpose and position.

In Hebrew thought, a name also equals a reputation. In English, we are not unfamiliar with this concept. We will talk about someone whose "name" can be trusted with a loan or assignment. Years ago, one would make a contract with a handshake because the persons involved would depend upon the reputation (name) of the other and a handshake was as good as a signature. (Oh, to see those days again!) One may consider the name of a company to be worthy of trust. We speak of a "good name," meaning some entity or person being worthy of trust. The opposite is also true. When someone has a "bad name," it is nearly impossible to retrieve a good reputation. Sometimes a name must be changed in order to start fresh.

Some people have had their name changed by YHVH. Avram (Abram), meaning "exalted father" was changed to Avraham (Abraham), meaning "father of many." Y'akov (Jacob) meaning "supplanter" was changed to Yisrael (Israel), meaning "he who strives or contends with El (God)." Their destiny was changed when their names were changed. I have experienced this name change in my own life as well as seen it prophetically in other's lives.

There is a story of Napoleon Bonaparte going to visit prisoners in a jail in France during the war. He came upon a young man and asked his name. The young man said his name was Napoleon. The emperor and commander of the army, Napoleon, said to the young man. "Young man, either change your name or change your conduct!"

I believe we are in an age when it is time to change "Jesus Christ" back to His original Hebrew name "Yeshua HaMashiach" or "Yeshua the Messiah" in order to restore the reputation of the One who was sent to be the Deliverer of Israel and a Light to the Nations (Goyim). I have come to believe that when Yeshua's Hebrew name was lost in the forming of the Christian religion, both Jewish people and Christians were deprived of the full meaning of His Name in the Scriptures. I have known Jewish people who did not even know that "Jesus" was Jewish (and unfortunately many more Christians who also do not know)! It is sad, but the history of the Christian religion shows us that Yeshua's Hebrew name and meaning were lost in translation., As a result, he was "gentilized." (We will explore this history in subsequent chapters.)

However, there is a specific reason why YHVH's plan was for Messiah to be Jewish! The scarlet thread of YHVH's plan to redeem mankind is seen in every book of the TaNaKH. We see it first in Genesis chapter 3 when Havah (Eve) is told that the serpent would "bruise his [Yeshua's] heel" but "he [Yeshua] would crush his [the serpent's] head."[3]

Reading on in the Scriptures, we see that YHVH chose Abraham, then Isaac, then Jacob, then Judah, and after many generations, David to be the line of Messiah. The Gospel book of Matthew begins with the genealogy of Yeshua. It affirms His heritage. YHVH also chose a people, Israel to be His bride, His representative or ambassador to the world. He asked them to be Holy as He is Holy. YHVH knows that the sacrificial system would never fully take care of the sin of mankind. He set up a plan to redeem all flesh through a spotless lamb. Yeshua became that spotless lamb. He became our "salvation" which is what His Name means!

But then His Name was changed and it no longer holds this meaning. In fact, it holds no intrinsic meaning in itself at all. And anyone who has spent any time at all in church history will attest to the appalling reputation of the "church" in regard to what has been done in the name of Jesus Christ. [4] So why the new name? And how could it be that such atrocities could be done using it?

Let's dig for a foundation stone in history and find some truth behind this name change.

We must first establish the historical setting of the birth of Yeshua.[5] He was born a few years before what is now known as the Common Era (C.E.) in the town of Beit Lechem (House of Bread - Bethlehem) in the area known as Judea in Israel. [6] He was of the Hebrew Israeli tribe of Judah and of the house of David. Therefore, He was fully Jewish. His earthly (not biological) father, Yosef (Joseph) and his mother Miryam (Mary) were betrothed. The Scriptures tell us that Miryam was visited by the angel Gavri'el (Gabriel whose name means "warrior of God") who announced to her that she would become pregnant by the Ruach HaKodesh (Holy Spirit) and would bear a Son, whom she was to name, Yeshua, because *"He will save His people from their sins."*[7] Yosef, being a righteous man, upon discovery that Miryam was pregnant, and not from him, wanted to "put her away quietly," but the same angel that appeared to Miryam, came to Yosef in a dream and told him not to be afraid because the child inside of her was from YHVH. The angel also confirmed to Yosef the Name by which he was to be called—Yeshua.[8]

Before Yeshua was born, another amazing birth took place, that of His cousin, Yochanan (John), whose name means "YHVH is gracious." Here we see the significance of the naming of a child in his story. (I have included the entire story of his birth because of the prophetic nature of his father's blessing when his voice was finally restored to him.)

On the eighth day, they came to do the child's b'rit-milah. They were about to name him Z'kharyah, after his father, when his mother spoke up and said, "No, he is to be called Yochanan." They said to her, "None of your relatives has that name," and they made signs to his father to find out what he wanted him called. He motioned for a writing tablet, and to everyone's surprise he wrote, "His name is Yochanan." At that moment, his power of speech returned, and his first words were a b'rakhah (blessing) to God. All their neighbors were awestruck; and throughout the hill country of Y'hudah, people talked about all these things. Everyone who heard of them said to himself, "What is this child going to be?" For clearly the hand of ADONAI was with him. His father Z'kharyah was filled with the Ruach HaKodesh and spoke this prophecy: "Praised be ADONAI, the God of Isra'el, because he has visited and made a ransom to liberate his people by raising up for us a mighty Deliverer who is a descendant of his servant David. It is just as he has spoken through the mouth of the prophets from the very beginning that we should be delivered from our enemies and from the power of all who hate us. "This has happened so that he might show the mercy promised to our fathers—that he would remember his holy covenant, the oath he swore before Avraham avinu to grant us that we, freed from our enemies, would serve him without fear, in holiness and righteousness before him all our days. You, child, will be called a prophet of Ha`Elyon;

you will go before the Lord to prepare his way by spreading the knowledge among his people that deliverance comes by having sins forgiven through our God's most tender mercy, which causes the Sunrise to visit us from Heaven, to shine on those in darkness, living in the shadow of death, and to guide our feet into the paths of peace." The child grew and became strong in spirit, and he lived in the wilderness until the time came for him to appear in public to Isra'el. (Luke 1:59-80)

There is great significance in the naming of a Jewish son. As we see in the Luke passage quoted at the beginning of this chapter, when Yeshua's parents had his B'rit Milah on the eighth day of His life on earth, He was named at that ceremony. It is possible that He was officially named "Yehoshua ben Yosef" (Joshua, son of Joseph) because the name "Yeshua" is an Aramaic form, or shortened form, of Yehoshua, whose name means "YHVH is a saving cry." [9] Aramaic was the common language of the people during the Second Temple period (the historical period from the post exile rebuilt Temple 530 BCE [10] to 70 CE). The Pashitta [11] (preserved Aramaic texts by the Eastern church) uses Yeshua as the Name for the Messiah. Among the Jews of the Second Temple period, the Biblical Aramaic/Hebrew name ישוע Yeshua was common: the Hebrew TaNaKH mentions several individuals with this name. This name is a feature of Biblical books written in the post-Exilic period (Ezra, Nehemiah, and Chronicles) and was found in the Dead Sea Scrolls.

In chapter 13 we will explore how the Name Yeshua is found in the Old Covenant Scriptures as the word "Salvation." The word for salvation ישועה yeshua is the feminine form of ישע yasha, a primary root: *to be open, wide, or free, to be safe, to free, defend, deliver, help, preserve, rescue, bring salvation, get victory.* Yeshua, as a Name, means יהוה [YHVH – the personal Name of Elohim (God)] is our salvation, deliverance, aid, victory, prosperity, health, and help. His Name has an amazing reputation and when you get to know Him personally, you will find that He is true to His Name.

----

[1] "Torah 101 – The Name of God" from Mechon Mamre (Hebrew for "Mamre Institute"), Jerusalem, Israel, mechon-mamre.org, http://www.mechon-mamre.org/jewfaq/name.htm. (I did a study, one time, on the usage of the word "name" in the Scriptures. I hand-wrote 30 pages of Scriptures that specifically spoke of the use of YHVH's and Yeshua's Names! It became such a revelation of the importance of His Name. The Jewish people will use "HaShem" instead of any form of pronunciation of YHVH. It literally means "The Name." Although, as I stated before, I believe the "personal" Name of God has been "lost" in translated Scriptures, I understand and honor the use of HaShem. The above referenced study goes into much detail.)

[2] Asher Intrater, Revive-Israel.org, "Anointing of the Prophets" Session 2, Oct.12, 2012 (available on ITunes).

[3] Genesis 3:15

[4] If you are a "Christian" and have never explored church history, it is time you took a walk down history lane and become aware of the realities of your heritage. I took a four-credit church history course in seminary, but I was given a Gentile Christian view of it. I never learned some of the real history, sad to say, but I do remember being very annoyed and upset by what I did learn. I remember thinking "we" had done a pretty bad job over the centuries. Brad Scott gives a very good summary in his message "The History of the Church: on the ROCK or on the rocks?" on his, *WildBranch Ministry* website (wildbranch.org). You can find it by searching for "History of the Church" on his site or by going to this link: http://www.wildbranch.org/marketplace/index.php?main_page=product_info&products_id=67 (We will also discuss some church history in chapters 9 and 10.)

[5] The Bible is considered to be a verifiable historical book. The fact of Yeshua's existence is not in question nor will we be trying to "prove" the accuracy of the Biblical text in regards to His birth, death, and resurrection.

There are plenty of wonderful resources to explore these issues from all sides. The purpose of this book does not cover that. I come from a belief and establishment that the B'rit Hadasha (New Covenant) Scriptures are factual, historical, inspired writings in equal standing to the writings of the Old Covenant.

[6] It is my firm belief that Yeshua was not born on Christmas day, December 25th of any year. First of all, there was no Gregorian Calendar during the time Yeshua lived on the earth. Secondly, winter was not the time of year when "Shepherds were abiding in their fields and watching their flocks." Thirdly, everything Yeshua fulfilled, He did on a "Feast of YHVH," not a Gregorian calendar date or pagan holiday. We are to celebrate His life, death, and resurrection during the "Feasts of YHVH" already prescribed for us in the Scriptures. Is it "wrong" to celebrate the birth of Yeshua? You must search the Scriptures, ask the Father, and make a decision based on spirit and truth. It is never wrong to worship YHVH, the Son, or the Ruach. We must be aware and willing to obey His voice.

[7] Luke 1:26-38

[8] Matthew 1:18-25

[9] Various sources were used to summarize this history of Yeshua's Name. The Wikipedia page on Yeshua documents these facts as well as David Stern's *Jewish New Testament Commentary*, Jewish New Testament Publications, Clarksville, Maryland, 1992, pp. 4–5.

[10] Judaism uses CE (Common Era) instead of AD, and BCE (Before the Common Era) is used instead of BC.

[11] The *Pashitta*, which was written and preserved as an Aramaic/Syriac text since at least the fifth century is thought by some to be the original text of the New Testament Gospels. The controversy over whether the New Testament writers wrote in Aramaic or Greek continues on. Whether the Pashitta is from the original apostles or not, the fact remains that the Aramaic script uses Yeshua as the Name and did not use the Greek Ἰησοῦς *Iēsoûs*. For more information on the Pashitta see: *Aramaic English New Testament* (AENT), Netzari Press LLC Mount Vernon, WA or: http://en.wikipedia.org/wiki/Peshitta or http://en.wikipedia.org/wiki/Aramaic_New_Testament

6

Something Got Lost in the Transliteration

So I turned myself and my thoughts to know,
search out and seek wisdom and the reasons
behind things, also to know how foolish it
is to be wicked and how stupid to act like a
fool. ... This is the only thing I have found,
that God made human beings upright,
but they have devised many schemes.
(Ecclesiastes 7:25,29)

My Aunt Bette is 90 years old. About two years ago we
were visiting with her in her home in Pennsylvania. Aunt Bette
has gone to church all of her life and would consider herself a
"Christian." As we were sharing at the lunch table, I mentioned
that Jesus' true name was Yeshua. She was shocked! She had
never heard that before and as I shared about His Hebrew/
Jewish roots she began to cry and ask if she was even "saved"
because she never knew that! It caused her to question if there
were other things she had been taught over those many years
in church that may have been wrong. We assured her that
knowing the original name of her Savior was not a prerequisite
for salvation.[1]

I am aware of all the groups who are trying to come up
with a perfect pronunciation and spelling of both the names of
YHVH and Yeshua. I am not going to get into pronunciations
or spellings. I have no intention of adding to an already out
of control controversy. I am more concerned with history,
meanings, and reputation. An exact pronunciation is not the

"spirit" of what the Spirit of YHVH is trying to bring about in these days. He is more concerned with your heart then political correctness!

There are three words in the English Bible that appear from time to time. "Then man began....." [2] It seems to be true that when YHVH sets up a plan, *then man begins* to add, subtract, distort, change, and come up with his own plan. YHVH must wonder as He observes mankind taking what is intended to be good and pure and making a mess out of it! (Romans 1 is a good study of this.) The most devastating of these messes has been RELIGION! As I shared before, I believe religion is man made, not YHVH's plan! So, how did we ever get from Yeshua (or even Yehoshua) to Jesus?

The study of language is a fascinating enterprise. I have traveled in several countries that speak another language from my own. The "tower of Babel" becomes reality when trying to simply get from "A to B" and especially when trying to communicate on a deeper level. I have only been able to learn one other language fairly well—good enough to understand jokes, pray, and have a deeper conversation. That language is Holland Dutch. I lived there with my first husband and daughters in the mid 80's while serving with YWAM (Youth with a Mission). I quickly discerned that language is far more than words or an exchange of words. It is all wrapped up in culture. Western culture may seem to be similar among various countries, but I was amazed how different the Dutch culture was from my own American one and how wrapped up in language that culture was expressed! There are still words, to this day, that I would prefer to say in Dutch rather than English because one just can't translate it well enough.

When we look at a language such as Hebrew, we see many challenges to the western reader. The written language

SOMETHING GOT LOST IN THE TRANSLITERATION

structure goes from right to left, instead of left to right. The characters are completely different and the vowels are usually missing! Plus add the cultural context! The Hebrew mindset is completely diverse from a Western Greek mindset. In all the visits we have made to Israel, I have tried to learn conversational Hebrew.³ Yet I find it difficult to understand the common person on the street. I can formulate my own sentence, but when they give an answer—well let's just say, "It all sounds "Greek" to me!" Speaking of Greek—hmmm—that is the subject we are going to "dig" into next.

In my study of history, I have learned about the "Hellenistic" period.⁴ The Hellenistic influence took place in the time period of ancient Greek history that centers around Alexander the Great (356-323 BCE) and the subsequent emergence of the Roman Empire which conquered all of the Near East, Middle East, and Southwestern Asia and lasted all the way until the mid fifteenth century. Its influence is still embedded in our western culture. The Greek/Roman influence in culture, language, arts, religion, government, and philosophy transformed whole regions of the known world at that time. Hellenism means "imitation of the Greeks" and the influence of this imitation transformed a great number of Jewish people of the time period preceding the birth of Yeshua. In fact, as a result of this Greek influence, between 300 and 200 BCE, the Hebrew TaNaKH was translated into Greek because a number of Jewish people had lost their use of the Hebrew language and their desire was to have something in the common vernacular of the times. This translation is well known as the "Septuagint."

During this same period of time a terrible thing happened in post exile Israel. For the Jews who had returned from Babylon between 536 and 432 BCE, Greek Hellenism became something that permeated every area of society. By the time Antiochus Epiphanes (whose name means "god manifest") came into power, there was great pressure for all Jewish people to convert to a Greek culture and language. In

45

fact, under his reign, such conversion was forced and Jews were required to abandon their Jewish practices and eat pork, which is considered an abomination and is against the Torah commandments. Antiochus even erected an altar to Jupiter in the Temple and sacrificed a pig on it, thereby desecrating the altar and the Temple. He did everything in his power to obliterate the Jewish religion.

[I need to make a note here that the adversary (satan)[5] has been trying to annihilate the Jewish people since "time began" and he uses many of the same tactics over and over again. We will see these same tactics later in history when the "Christians" begin to align themselves with him and not with YHVH. Unfortunately, we see these same tactics repeating themselves in our days.]

During this time a group of Jews, under the leadership of Matthias Maccabee, began to revolt and reclaim their position as Hebrew Jews in the region. They were fearless warriors who did not bow down to the reign of Antiochus or his demands. YHVH gave them power and victory over their enemies. In 165 BCE they reclaimed the Temple, restored, and rededicated it to YHVH. The story of Hannukah (Feast of Dedication) was inaugurated to commemorate this victory, and is celebrated to this day in the Hebrew month of Kislev. Yeshua even celebrated this feast.[6]

Are you aware of this holiday and its origins? It is a great story of bravery, warfare against an evil dictator, and victory with the power and hand of YHVH behind them, defeating their enemies who far outnumbered them.[7]

What does this have to do with Yeshua's name? Well, the Greek influence of that period of time continued well into the first centuries of the Common Era and the writing of the New Covenant Scriptures (B'rit Hadashah). Even though there is good evidence of a "Hebrew Matthew," most older versions of the New Covenant have only been preserved in Greek. (The Eastern Orthodox church maintains that the Aramaic Pashitta is the oldest, most original form of the New Covenant Scriptures – see p. 42, footnote 11). I will dig into the history of the early followers of the "Way" in the following chapters, but first I want to finish telling what happened to Yeshua's name.

When doing a translation of something, most words in the text are translated. The meaning gets transferred from the source language to the target language in the best way possible to maintain the same idea or concept. Sometimes a "literal translation" can sound odd in the target language, so translators may paraphrase a sentence to make the concept clear to the reader. Grammar and syntax are difficult to maintain between very different language groups because of their structures. That is why scholars like to study texts in their original languages. There are often things "lost in translation." (We'll get to that in the next chapter).

Names tend to be transliterated, not translated. To transliterate something, you are simply taking the sound of the letters from the source language and attempting to get a similar sound in the target language. You are not transferring meaning at all. This is why Yehoshua becomes Joshua. It is a similar sound using English letters. (In Old English, the "J" sounded like a "Y.") The most interesting part of the history of Biblical translation is what happened to names from the original Biblical texts as English evolved and became a predominant language, especially in the "Christian" world.

The translation of the Hebrew names in the TaNaKH to English sound similar to one another. If you read "Abraham" it sounds like אברהם "Avraham." יצחק "Yitzchak" sounds similar to "Isaac." [8]

Let's think about a few other things. The Jewish people have restored their Temple and language after the Maccabean revolt and victory. For over 150 years the common language among Jews in Judea is Hebrew and/or Aramaic. (although there remain some Greek speaking Jews as spoken of in the book of Acts.) Both Hebrew and Aramaic are from the Semitic

47

language root. Remember that language is very wrapped up in culture. The Hebrew culture and mindset were firmly established since the beginning of Biblical times and preserved in the writings of the Torah since the time of Moshe (Moses). (The Jewish people have meticulously preserved the Torah and writings of the TaNaKH for millennium! We owe a great gratitude to them for such a gift.)

So, Yeshua and His disciples spoke Hebrew and Aramaic. Whether the original texts of the Gospels and writings in the New Covenant were in Hebrew, Aramaic, or Greek, the fact remains that the English form of Yeshua's name came from the Greek and not from the Hebrew. Had it come from the Hebrew, He would most likely have become "Joshua." In fact, the most astounding fact, mostly unknown to current day English speakers, is that the hard "J" sound we currently use for a host of Biblical names such as Jeremiah, Joshua, Joseph, Joram, Jerusalem, and in names such as Elijah, is a recent addition to the English language.[9] The "j" as we know it today only came into usage in the 16th century, so in actual fact, the name "Jesus" is only 500 years old!!

Transliteration from one language to another, and then to another, is like a copy of a copy. It does not look (or sound) like the original at all!

Let's get back to the Greek. The Greek transliteration of Yeshua became Ἰησοῦς or Iēsoûs. There is no "sh" sound in Greek, which accounts for the middle "s" sound in Iesous. The "s" at the end of the Greek name is grammatically necessary for conjugation.[10] Therefore, when the Greek was transliterated to English, Iesous became Yesus, which eventually became Jesus. The same thing is true for the word "Christ" which has somehow become Yeshua's "last name" or surname. The word "Christ" is derived from the Greek Χριστός Khrīstos, meaning "anointed one," a translation of the Hebrew מָשִׁיחַ, (Mashiach) usually transliterated into English as "Messiah." In the Septuagint version of the Hebrew Bible (written two centuries before the time of Yeshua), the word "Khristos" was used to translate the Hebrew word "Messiah" (מָשִׁיחַ) into Greek. "Christ" became viewed as a name, one part of "Jesus Christ," but originally it was a title ("Jesus the Anointed").[11] What was lost in the transliteration was the **meaning** of His name. Transliteration never transfers meaning, only sounds. If translators had kept the meaning of Yeshua's name as Salvation, it would have been σωτηρία (sotaria or sotarios) in the Greek.[12] I prefer the name Yeshua!

Now that we know how the Name Yeshua became Jesus, you might be asking, "So, what does it matter?" Well, to answer that, we have to dig deeper into our excavation site into the history behind other changes. Are you willing to dig some more and get a little dirtier?

----

[1] I will never say that if you don't use the "right" name, you won't get into the Kingdom of Heaven. Heaven forbid! That is not Scriptural and does not represent the God I serve! It only "serves" to bring more division and "diversion" from the true Gospel!! I must ask — "Do I want to be Right? Or do I want to be Righteous?"

[2] I heard this once in a message or sermon, but cannot remember who said it. I would like to give credit where credit is due, so if you were the one I heard it from, thank you!

[3] Over the past decade we have traveled to Israel several times and stayed up to three months at a time on a tourist visa. Going without reservations, we have seen YHVH's divine appointments lead us to various places in the country and connections to amazing Jewish people we have come to know and love, who now call us "mishpacha" (family). We volunteered in a hostel in Jerusalem near the Old City, lived in Galilee in the home of a Jewish family twice, and lived in Jerusalem's Old City's Jewish and Christian Quarters. Our greatest desire would be to move to Israel permanently!

[4] http://en.wikipedia.org/wiki/Hellenistic_civilization as well as many other pages that stem from this one, including Hellenization and Hellenism. When I was in High School, history was my least favorite subject! Now I can't get enough of it! I want to learn more because when I dig and search for truth, I learn where what I believe came from.

[5] "Adversary" is the translation of the Hebrew word שטן – satan. Scripturally, satan was an archangel who was known as the "covering cherub" (see Isaiah 28:14,16). He rebelled and was thrown out of heaven with one third of the angels who joined him in his rebellion. He had a name, but was stripped of it. I do not capitalize satan because it is not a proper name – only a designation – which means "adversary."

[6] Yochanan - John 10:22

[7] The story of the Maccabees can be found in the Apocrypha books of I and II Maccabees as well as: http://www.mechon-mamre.org/jewfaq/holiday7.htm

[8] It is very interesting to note that the name "James" in our English Bibles comes from the name "Ya'akov" or what would normally be translated as Jacob, and is translated such in the Old Testament. However, in the New Testament the name James is used because King James, the inspiration behind an English version of the Bible wanted his own name to be used. I'll let you draw your own conclusions.

[9] The Hebrew and Aramaic languages do not have a hard "J" sound or letter representing that sound. History of the J - Wikipedia, the free encyclopedia. htm

[10] Botkin, Dr. Daniel, *The Messiah's Hebrew Name: "'Yeshua" Or "Yahshua"?* www.yashanet.com/library/Yeshua_or_Yahshua.htm

[11] www.wikipedia.org/wiki/Jesus

[12] Strong's Concordance G4991 and G4992

Something Got Lost in Translation

How happy are those whose way of life is blameless, who live by the Torah of Adonai! How happy are those who observe his instruction, who seek him wholeheartedly! ... I treasure your word in my heart, that I might not sin against you.... Open my eyes, so that I will see wonders from your Torah.... Teach me good judgment and knowledge, because I trust in your *mitzvot*. Before I was humbled, I used to go astray; but now I observe your word.... How I love your Torah! I meditate on it all day. I am wiser than my foes, because your *mitzvot* are mine forever.... Your word is a lamp for my foot and light on my path.... I hate double-minded people, but I love your Torah.... My eyes fail from watching for your salvation (yeshuah) and for [the fulfillment of] your righteous promise.... Your righteousness is eternal righteousness and your Torah is truth.... The pursuers of carnality are getting close; they are distancing themselves from your Torah.... The main thing about your word is that it's true; and all your just rulings last forever.... Those who love your Torah have great peace; nothing makes them stumble.... I long for your deliverance (yeshuah), Adonai; and your Torah is my delight. (Psalm 119: 1-2,18,66,97-98,123,142,150,160,165,174)

There are times when I receive an email or newsletter in Dutch from our friends in Holland. I understand what they are saying, but when I go to translate it to Ronald, I have a difficult time finding the correct English words to convey the concept that is being shared. I stumble and stutter trying to get it right. Even so, no matter how hard I try some things get lost in the translating. Sometimes there just are no English words that express the exact meaning and connotation.

In the same way, there are also several words in the Bible that have lost the depths of their meaning when translated from Hebrew to Greek or Hebrew to English. (You wonder why there are so many Bible translations in English??!!) This is where we encounter the age old problem of the Tower of Babel. "Babel" means "confusion." The scattering of people and the development of languages is truly vast and complicated, and often confusing! "Ethnologue" lists 6,909 living languages in the world![1] Only about 200 are major languages that cover about 94% of the world's population, but just think of the enormity of the task of communicating concepts and the challenges of translators.

I like to watch when the UN holds a session and everyone has their little headphones, listening to someone up in the sound box, translating the speech into their own language. If we thought "whisper down the lane" had the potential to change the origin of the message, just think of what happens when we translate to so many different people groups!

I can only imagine the challenges of the translators of the Bible! It would be an enormous task because of the sacred nature of the book. How does one preserve the context and content from a culture that is so foreign to us? Just think about 6000 years of history and how much culture has changed in that period of time. And yet..... what a miracle that the Scriptures have been preserved for such a long time and that the living, breathing, Word of YHVH continues to speak to us today! I find that to be one of the most amazing miracles. It proves to me that no matter what language or culture the Word is placed in, it will bring life.

"For my thoughts are not your thoughts, and your ways are not my ways," says ADONAI. "As high as the sky is above the earth are my ways higher than your ways, and my thoughts than your thoughts. For just as rain and snow fall from the sky and do not return there, but water the earth, causing it to bud and produce, giving seed to the sower and bread to the eater; so is my word that goes out from my mouth—it will not return to me unfulfilled; but it will accomplish what I intend, and cause to succeed what I sent it to do." (Isaiah 55:8-11)

However, there are times when a particular concept does get "lost in translation" because one word just can't capture the full and true meaning of the original. When that happens, it is possible for a whole doctrine to be built on the new concept. Developed over time, that doctrine may eventually be so far from the original, that it will be hard to reclaim or recover the intended meaning.

My husband used to work as a civil/mechanical engineer. For him, everything had to be level and square. When working on a job site, such as installing a paper machine, accuracy was essential. He worked in the measurements of two to three thousandths of an inch (the thickness of one hair strand)! He says "If you make a one degree mistake in an angle, in 100 feet you would be approximately 1 foot 9 inches off. That's a *big* mistake!" Just think of the NASA engineers trying to get to the moon. If they were off a small degree, the astronauts would have missed the moon!

If you think of a translation that started even 500 years ago that conveyed a certain meaning, what happens when that continues to "evolve" down through the ages? A big distortion can occur. To reclaim that difference can be enormous. Only the Spirit of YHVH can correct our path.

I really appreciate what David Stern, a Messianic Jewish believer, did when he produced the Complete Jewish Bible.[2] He had the wisdom to use transliterated Hebrew proper names throughout the entire Bible. In addition, when a word, such as *Torah,* which he believed could not be correctly translated as "law" was used, he would simply use the word *Torah.* He does this with several other words as well. In an essay he wrote for the book "How Jewish is Christianity," he says *"We...think it is high time to bring Yeshua back home where He belongs, where Jewish people can see him as a fellow Jew able to meet the need of every Jewish heart."*[3] I say "Amen" to that!

We will explore two particular word concepts in this chapter from the Hebrew Old Covenant (the TaNaKH) which I believe have taken on a different meaning in the English then was intended by the author (YHVH).

Torah: The verses listed at the beginning of the chapter are great examples of the use of the word "Torah" in the TaNaKH. The Hebrew word תורה "Torah" literally means *teaching* or *instruction.*[4] It includes the law of YHVH through Moshe (Moses), but it encompasses the entire first five books of the TaNaKH, which are commonly known among Christians as the Pentatuch (Penta – meaning "five"). In fact, Torah is a term used throughout the entire Bible because it is all instruction!

Because the word "Torah" has such a deeper and broader depth than the English translation "law," you can see how easy it may be to misinterpret its meaning, especially when you transfer it to a different culture and context from how it was originally presented. You see, Torah includes the whole history, from the beginning of time until the Israelites entered the Promised Land. It includes creation, Adam and Eve, the fall, Noah and the flood, the Tower of Babel, Abraham, Isaac, Jacob, Joseph, Moses, the Exodus, and the forty years in the wilderness. It is much more than law or rules. It is full of story and illustration, *and* instruction.

Have you ever asked yourself the question, "Why did YHVH sanctify the Sabbath *before* man ever fell into sin in the garden?" or "Why did Noah know which animals were "clean or unclean" before the laws were officially given that detailed clean and unclean animals?" You see, the Torah is much more than law. It is a treasure chest of directions and instructions that YHVH gave to man because He loves us so much and knows what is best for us. Like a Father who is wise and wonderful, we can't help but love Him back!

We had the privilege of visiting a special shop in the Jewish Quarter of the Old City of Jerusalem. The shop is called "Shorashim" (meaning "roots").[5] There Moshe and Dov take the time to gather tour groups of Christians to give them a Jewish perspective on things that Christians have always assumed about Jews, the Bible, and the culture they are visiting. It is a wonderful service they are performing.

We were visiting at a time when a group of Christians were stuffed into the little shop like sardines. Moshe shared that one time when his wife was pregnant, she had a craving for an orange. It was late in the evening, but Moshe took it upon himself to go and find her an orange. As he searched the city for an open shop, he found one and carefully scrutinized the oranges. He not only wanted to find the best orange for her, but he wanted to find a dozen of the best oranges for her because he loved her! Even though she probably only ate one, he showered her with the best. It was an act of love.

So it is, he said, with following the Torah. We want to give our best to YHVH because we love Him, not because we drudgingly have to! I love the perspective Moshe gave to us that day.

Yeshua said that the greatest commandment was this *"Shema, Israel. Adonai Elohenu. Adonai Echad" (Hear, O Israel. Adonai is God. Adonai is One) and you shall love Adonai Your God with all your heart, all your being, and with all your resources...* (D'varim – Deuteronomy 6:4-5).[6] Then Yeshua said the second is like it. *"You shall love your neighbor as yourself"* (Vayikra – Leviticus 19:18). How can we love YHVH? With our whole heart, being, and resources! Do we do things out of obligation or drudgery? Or do we do them because we love Him so much we just can't help ourselves?

I want to be so in love with YHVH and Yeshua that it gives me great delight to observe Torah! I am not "under" the compulsion to obey the law—I get to! I am at liberty and in liberty through the Blood of Yeshua because He gave me the Spirit of Truth to help me understand Torah and the depths of YHVH's Plan for all of us!

What if we had the perspective that Torah is not laws or legalism, but freedom and blessing? What if we saw the very heart of YHVH in giving us instructions that would only enhance our lives and not diminish them? Legalism is what happens when we take what YHVH has shown us and force it upon another. It is what happens when we forget that YHVH is the author and finisher of our faith and the faith of our "brother or sister", or when we forget where we ourselves came from and what YHVH redeemed us from! We prescribe what and how and who instead of affirming and encouraging and blessing. Grace is not a New Covenant concept.

Part of the foundation that has been lacking in most Christian churches is the Old Covenant Scriptures. Most Christians like to pick and choose. I have heard people say "I like the Psalms, but I don't like Leviticus!" "I don't like to read the Old Testament. It's too bloody" or "I don't understand it" or "I don't like the God of the Old Testament, I like Jesus." or "We don't need the Old Testament. Everything we need is from the Cross on!"

Without the "ancient paths," the New Covenant Scriptures have no depth and no foundation. Religion becomes shallow. You don't really know YHVH without it because you have made Him something you can put in a box. The building is very weak because there is no solid foundation.

In the same manner, I personally know a Jewish man who came to faith in Yeshua without having ever read the New Testament! Through revelation by the Spirit, it is all there. YHVH will reveal Himself and His plan of redemption if we will just look for it. *"Not by Might, Not by Power, but by My Spirit says the Lord!"* (Zechariah 4:6 KJV)

We need the Torah and the Old Covenant Scriptures to grapple with the hard questions and mysteries. We need to seek YHVH for the whys. We need to see the pattern of Israel before us and examine our own foolishness. We need to hear the prophets screaming to us in this day with the same message.

May I challenge you to read the TaNaKh Scriptures, not "just to get through them," but really seeking to know the YHVH of those Scriptures and asking Him to open the eyes of your understanding?

My husband and I go through the Parashah readings each week which are portions of the Torah in a cycle from Genesis to Deuteronomy each year.[7] Every time we read through them, we marvel at how fresh and new the portion of Scripture is that we are studying. That is what the living, breathing, Word of YHVH is. It should be fresh and new to us each day and speaking to us personally.

When you read the B'rit Hadashah (New Covenant), you must realize that the only Scripture available to the reader of that time was the TaNaKH (Old Testament). The New Covenant did not exist! There were writings, but they were not "canonized" until the fourth century, so they were not considered "Scripture." [8]

See, the Word of God is alive! It is at work and is sharper than any double-edged sword—it cuts right through to where soul meets spirit and joints meet marrow, and it is quick to judge the inner reflections and attitudes of the heart. Before God, nothing created is hidden, but all things are naked and open to the eyes of him to whom we must render an account. (Hebrews 4:12-13)

Yeshua said:

"Don't think that I have come to abolish the Torah or the Prophets. I have come not to abolish, but to complete. Yes indeed! I tell you that until heaven and earth pass away, not so much as a yud or a stroke will pass from the Torah—not until everything that must happen has happened. So, whoever disobeys the least of these mitzvot and teaches others to do so will be called the least in the Kingdom of Heaven. But whoever obeys them and so teaches will be called great in the Kingdom of Heaven. For I tell you, that unless your righteousness is far greater than that of the Torah-teachers and P'rushim, you will certainly not enter the Kingdom of Heaven!"
(Matthew 5:17-20)

We see a complete picture of the purposes of YHVH through His Son. Yeshua was sent to "complete and fulfill" the Torah and is encouraging us to teach others to obey it. Reading the Gospel accounts with new eyes, you will see that the Torah of Moshe was difficult but Yeshua's was far more stringent. Ask the Ruach (Spirit) to give you new eyes to see Yeshua's version of the Torah. He divides "bone from marrow" when He says, "You have heard.... But I say...." In other words, He gets to the heart, the intentions of man. Can you look into your own heart and examine yourself? Why would Yeshua's Torah (instruction) be more demanding than Moshe's? What does this mean for believers today?

For a child is born to us, a son is given to us; dominion will rest on his shoulders, and he will be given the name Pele-Yo'etz El Gibbor Avi-'Ad Sar-Shalom. (Isaiah 9:5(6))

A person whose desire rests on you, you preserve in perfect peace, (Hebrew "shalom, shalom") because he trusts in you. (Isaiah 26:3)

"What I am leaving with you is shalom—I am giving you my shalom. I don't give the way the world gives. Don't let yourselves be upset or frightened."
(John 14:27)

Shalom: Shalom is translated "Peace" in English and is commonly defined as "the absence of conflict." Its true translation is: *completeness, soundness, safety, welfare, peace, health, prosperity, tranquility, contentment, wholeness.*[9] To me, this is a far deeper and encompassing definition—one that makes me just feel good all over!

I grew up in Lancaster County, Pennsylvania among the Amish and Mennonites. I was a part of the Mennonite denomination for a portion of my adult life. I was initially drawn to their "peace" stance and believed they had a very profound view of the use of non-violence to resolve conflicts. I have come to realize that every belief, temperament, and gifting has both strengths and weaknesses. I have seen this

in the "Anabaptist" movement. The strength of their stance
is that their views challenge us to consider reconciliation and
conflict resolution. *"Blessed are the peace makers,"* Yeshua
said (Matthew 5:9). There is a place and time for making peace.
(Did He mean "shalom makers"?)

The weakness is that some have come to believe in peace
above all, making it man-made—bloodless, thereby negating or
circumventing the holiness of YHVH. It is another "distancing
from Torah." I am not saying all of them have diverted from
the truth of the Word of God. However, the tendency has arisen
because of the definition of a word. Their definition does not
align with a Hebrew mindset and culture, which houses the
foundation of the Biblical meaning of peace—shalom. In fact,
in many cases their "tolerance" and acceptance of all peoples
and religions has caused a shift from a Biblical foundation to a
foundation of sand.

"Shalom" is also a greeting. It is a blessing. When you
are speaking shalom to someone, you are giving so much more
than peace. In speaking shalom over people, you give them
a complete blessing. I have prayed over people and spoken
shalom over them and seen the breath of YHVH just wash
them from head to foot. YHVH said this was a way to put His
name on Israel.

**"Speak to Aharon and his sons, and tell them that
this is how you are to bless the people of Isra'el:
you are to say to them, 'Y'varekh'kha ADONAI
v'yishmerekha. [May ADONAI bless you and keep
you.] Ya'er ADONAI panav eleikha vichunekka.
[May ADONAI make his face shine on you and
show you his favor.] Yissa ADONAI panav eleikha
v'yasem l'kha shalom. [May ADONAI lift up his
face toward you and give you peace.]' In this way**

they are to put my name on the people of Isra'el, so that I will bless them." (Numbers 6:23-27)

Now perhaps you can see how easy it is for cults and false teaching to develop because of a diversion from the Hebrew root/foundation. There are many more examples of this, but we will stop here. Some things definitely got "lost in translation." Are you willing to find more lost treasures?

----

[1] http://www.ethnologue.com/statistics/area

[2] David H. Stern, *The Complete Jewish Bible,* Jewish New Testament Publications, Inc., Clarksville, MD, 1998.

3 Goldberg, Louis, editor, *How Jewish is Christianity?* David H. Stern, "Summary Essay: The Future of Messianic Judaism," Zondervan, Grand Rapids, MI, 2003.

[4] Strong's Exhaustive Concordance – H8451 www.blueletterbible.org

[5] http://www.shorashim.com/

[6] The Hebrew word for God is Elohim. This is a plural word. Embedded in the Hebrew concept of God as a being with different roles and "parts." Genesis 1:26 "Let us make man in *our* image." The Christian concept of "trinity" is originally from this idea of God being a "plural" being. Therefore the idea of "echad" in the Hebrew, meaning "together" or "unity" instead of one, as in number, is an embedded Hebrew concept of the Father, Son, and Holy Spirit.

[7] Every Jewish synagogue, worldwide, uses the same portions of the Torah Scriptures each week called a "Parashah" reading. The cycle begins at the end of the Feast of Tabernacles (Sukkot) on a special holiday called "Simcha Torah" (Rejoicing over the Torah). Even in the time of Yeshua, there were weekly readings from the Torah and the Prophets (called Haftorah readings). See Luke 4:16-21.

[8] Peter speaks highly of Paul's (Sha'ul) letters when he says in II Peter 3:15-16 *"And think of our Lord's patience as deliverance, just as our dear brother Sha'ul also wrote you, following the wisdom God gave him. Indeed, he speaks about these things in all his letters. They contain some things that are hard to understand, things which the uninstructed and unstable distort, to their own destruction, as they do the other Scriptures."* This seems to indicate that the letters of Paul were widely known and accepted as "wisdom from God," but not as "Scriptures" because here Peter even separates the two, referring to "the Scriptures" as "other." I am not saying the New Covenant is not "Scripture" as inspired by the Holy Spirit. I am stating the fact that they were not "Scriptures" at the time they were written. The Hebrew TaNaKH is the foundation of the Word of YHVH. The New Covenant shows us the Word becoming Flesh through Yeshua. The writings of the New Covenant are "torah" instruction to believers and I believe come as wisdom from YHVH.

[9] Strong's H7965 – Just a side note: Did you know that the phrase "Peace on Earth" is nowhere in the Bible? The correct translation is "On Earth Peace." I see a big difference between the two phrases. Yeshua came "on earth" as "Peace (Shalom)" – There will only be "Peace on Earth" when He comes to restore rule and reign as King of Kings and Lord of Lords, and if I may say so, He will not be coming "peacefully"!

8

A Treasure Hunt

Yes, if you will call for insight and raise your voice for discernment, if you seek it as you would silver and search for it as for hidden treasure—then you will understand the fear of ADONAI and find knowledge of God. For ADONAI gives wisdom; from his mouth comes knowledge and understanding.

(Proverbs 2:3-6)

"But, as the Tanakh says, 'No eye has seen, no ear has heard and no one's heart has imagined all the things that God has prepared for those who love him.' It is to us, however, that God has revealed these things. How? Through the Spirit. For the Spirit probes all things, even the profoundest depths of God. For who knows the inner workings of a person except the person's own spirit inside him? So too no one knows the inner workings of God except God's Spirit. Now we have not received the spirit of the world but the Spirit of God, so that we might understand the things God has so freely given us. These are the things we are talking about when we avoid the manner of speaking that human wisdom would dictate and instead use a manner of speaking taught by the Spirit, by which we explain things of the Spirit to people who have the Spirit. Now the natural man does not receive the things from the Spirit of God - to him they are nonsense!

> Moreover, he is unable to grasp them, because
> they are evaluated through the Spirit. But the
> person who has the Spirit can evaluate everything,
> while no one is in a position to evaluate him. For
> who has known the mind of ADONAI? Who will
> counsel him? But we have the mind of the Messiah!
>
> (I Corinthians 2:9-15)

When I was the Transaction Manager at a Credit Union in Virginia, I went to a security seminar. There the instructor told us the best way to identify a counterfeit bill. It was to study the original. He said that the only way to know if a bill is counterfeit or not is to know the features of the original bill so well that when a counterfeit comes into your hands, you will know it immediately!

We need to apply this principle to the Word of YHVH and to Yeshua. Seek to know the original, to know the source, to know the Person! Do not be content to accept what you read or hear from the pulpit, radio, television, or the internet (or even this book). One of the best things that happened to me when Ronald and I moved to Maine over a decade ago, was that I was forced, for a period of time, to rely totally on the Bible and my relationship with YHVH. I had no church, no radio, television, or even books. The Father "weaned" me from my religious background because He wanted me to discover Him with fresh eyes and ears. He wanted me to know Him, not know about Him. He wanted me to study the "original" so that I would be able to discern, in this difficult time, that which is from/of Him and that which is counterfeit! I would encourage a new believer to spend their first year reading the Bible, praying, and learning how to listen to the voice of YHVH and then obeying Him.

How can we know what truth is? We have to get to the source of Truth and find out! Who is the source of truth?

YHVH, through His Ruach—His Spirit. Yeshua said He was *"the Way, the Truth, and the Life"* (John 14:6). He said to the woman at the well that there was a time coming when we would worship Him *"in Spirit and in Truth"* (John 4). The two go together. You can't have one without the other. You must have both. I have heard it said, "If you have only Spirit, you'll blow up. If you have only Truth, you'll dry up!" The Presence of YHVH is the only place to get both.

In the last chapter we explored a few words that have lost their full meaning in the translation. Now we will search for other things that have been lost. Let us be like the woman in Luke 15 who has lost a very special coin. She lights a lamp, sweeps the house and searches all over until she finds it (Luke 15:8). I'm getting excited already!

These are the designated times of ADONAI, the holy convocations you are to proclaim at their designated times. (Leviticus 23:4)

Did you know that YHVH has His own calendar? He is, of course, beyond, or "outside" time and space because He is so much ***more***, but He has chosen to confine man to time and has arranged creation so that days and months and seasons would be signs for us.

God said, "Let there be lights in the dome of the sky to divide the day from the night; let them be for signs, seasons, days and years." (Genesis 1:14)

As I have explored the calendar of YHVH I have been amazed at His infinite wisdom in arranging events based on these principles. It is important to note, because I never knew this myself until recent years, that YHVH's calendar is a lunisolar calendar. It is based on the cycle of the moon but adjusts to fit the seasonal rotation of the sun.[1] The Gregorian calendar is a solar calendar, based solely on the earth's cycle around the sun. The Hebrew year has two beginnings—a spiritual beginning and a civil beginning.

**You are to begin your calendar with this month;
it will be the first month of the year for you.**
(Exodus 12:2)

This is the beginning of the spiritual year. YHVH said this to Moshe (Moses) as He was preparing the tenth plague on Egypt, the death of all the first-born, which would usher in their deliverance from Egypt and from slavery. This month is the one known as Aviv (the Hebrew word for "spring") or Nissan (Hebrew for "miracles"). Biblically, months are numbered. Names of the months became common after the Babylonian exile and had a Chaldean influence.[2]

All Hebrew months begin on a "new moon." The new moon was announced by the sounding of the shofar. The priests assigned to this task were to watch carefully for the sighting of the new moon from the Temple Mount in Jerusalem. They truly did not know the "day or the hour." That is why it was announced with the shofar. Today we have it all calculated out for us at the "click of a mouse" or app on our IPad or IPhone!

The way YHVH ordered the event of the Exodus is something that never "dawned" on me until one year when I was observing the sky on Passover, I thought, "Of course YHVH would have a full moon for the Passover. They needed the light of the moon to leave in the middle of the night!" I'm sure I am not the only person to have been ignorant of this! I am just ashamed that I did not pay attention to these kinds of details before. They have been there, before my very eyes— just veiled.

The civil year begins on the first day of the seventh month. That day is the Feast of Trumpets—Rosh Hashana (Head of the

Year). Two weeks later, on another full moon, the Feast of Tabernacles—Sukkot begins, which is to be a remembrance of the Israelite's time in the wilderness. The booths or sukkot that are erected for that Feast must be constructed in such a way that when looking up through the branches, one can see the moon and stars.

The Calendar of YHVH is so fascinating and full of many hidden treasures. For example, in Jewish tradition, each month has a particular set of blessings and is designated to one of the twelve tribes of Israel. Although I do not subscribe to the Jewish mystical teachings associated with the months, I believe there is much more we can gain from learning about them. Jonathan Cahn, author of *The Harbinger* often refers to events that happen on particular Hebrew calendar days which we often miss because we are out of touch with YHVH's calendar.[3] Have you ever noticed this verse in Isaiah 66? *"Every month on Rosh-Hodesh (new moon)and every week on Shabbat, everyone living will come to worship in my presence," says ADONAI* (Isaiah 66:23). To me, this indicates that YHVH's calendar has eternal purposes!

The most special day on YHVH's calendar happens every week. Many Jewish people claim it as the "holiest day of the year," every week! I have already mentioned that YHVH sanctified the Sabbath, the weekly day of rest, before Adam and Eve sinned in the garden.[4]

In the Hebrew culture and in Biblical language there are only numbered days, just like the months. What we call Sunday is "Day 1." Monday is "Day 2," and so on.[5] A Hebrew day starts in the evening at sundown. That is because YHVH set it up that way in Genesis chapter 1. By the first verse of Genesis 2, YHVH is finished with creation and He sets up a rest day. He "sanctifies" (makes Holy) the seventh day. The word "Shabbat" comes from the Hebrew word for "seventh." We use the English word "Sabbath." The Hebrew letter ב "bet" can either be a "b" or a "v" and so you can get "Sabbath" from "Seventh," very easily in a transliteration.[6] The fourth commandment reads:

> **Remember the day, Shabbat, to set it apart for God. You have six days to labor and do all your work, but the seventh day is a Shabbat for ADONAI your God. On it, you are not to do any kind of work—not you, your son or your daughter, not your male or female slave, not your livestock, and not the foreigner staying with you inside the gates to your property. For in six days, ADONAI made heaven and earth, the sea and everything in them; but on the seventh day he rested. This is why ADONAI blessed the day, Shabbat, and separated it for himself. (Exodus 20:8-11)**

Who was the Sabbath made for? For YHVH! It is another one of the "love" Scriptures that we often miss. To understand the Sabbath you must understand its purpose. It is to delight yourself in YHVH! The rest of the days we are focused on work, on chores, on preparing food, and shopping for our needs. We are easily distracted from our spiritual devotion. We may take a few moments a day to read the Word or pray, but for the most part our days are filled with activity and work to provide for our basic needs. So, YHVH set apart a day to "cease striving" and get to know Him! We "bring in" Shabbat as a way to separate the profane from the sacred. We end the work week and we begin a feast! The above quoted Scripture from Isaiah 66 is referring to eternal time. The Sabbath and the New Moon (Rosh Hodesh) will continue on, even after the "Day of the Lord."

Over eleven years ago, Ronald and I were preparing for our first trip to Israel. We wanted to know what the Father required of us in our preparation. The first thing He required was for us to begin to observe the Biblical Sabbath. I grew up in mainstream Christianity and so Sunday was my normal day of worship and had always been. We said "yes sir" when we received the command to change. We had no idea what to do or how to do it. So we said "Let's read the Bible." (Do I hear someone saying "Duh!"?)

We studied the original. Every place it talked about the Sabbath we made a note of it. The first thing we discovered is that it started on Friday at sundown. Okay. Step 1. Then we noticed that we weren't to do any work on it. Okay. Step 2. We continued our search and began to observe it in the simple way we could, just following the step by step instructions in the Word of YHVH.

We began to notice two things. The first thing we noticed was how much our bodies enjoyed the Sabbath! We were getting some real rest! Sabbath is the key that unlocks the rest - both the rest of mind and body as well as the "rest of the story"!

The second thing we noticed is how much opposition we received from family and friends because we were doing it! It was amazing to us. But, we continued to follow the command of our all wise and knowing Father. It was easy to understand the Sabbath in Israel because we had already been observing it before we arrived. When we had our second sojourn there, we were living in an all-Jewish town in the Galilee. Through amazing Divine Appointments we were invited to an Orthodox Jewish home to celebrate Shabbat. That was the most wonderful evening! The children were all around the table and when the prayers and blessings were being said—all in Hebrew— we began to see the transformation on everyone's faces and the glow of the Spirit of YHVH pouring in. The singing and the laughter and the sharing of food that kept coming and coming…. Wow!

We left with a completely new appreciation and understanding of the Sabbath than we could have ever imagined. There was something so sacred and special about it. We felt like we had touched heaven. We were humbled by our own arrogance in thinking that Jewish people have "missed it." No, we had missed it!! It brings tears to my eyes, even today, ten years later. As I was observing this family, the Lord said to me concerning the 16-year-old girl that I was about to tutor in English, "She is mine." He said it with such pride and joy.

There are two important Hebrew words used in Leviticus 23 which details the Feasts of YHVH. The first word is מוֹעֵד "Moed" or plural – "moedim." The word means *an appointed time, appointed meeting.* The second word is מִקְרָא "mikra," which is translated "Holy Convocation." Its definition is – *assembly, a calling together, a reading.* Some see "rehearsal" in its meaning.[7] What are the Sabbath and the other Feasts of Adonai appointed times and rehearsals for? The Bible tells us they are for all generations—for eternity!

O the depth of the riches and the wisdom and knowledge of God! How inscrutable are his judgments! How unsearchable are his ways! For, "Who has known the mind of the Lord? Who has been his counselor?" Or, "Who has given him anything and made him pay it back?" For from him and through him and to him are all things. To him be the glory forever! Amen. (Romans 11:33-36)

These seven appointed times are: Pesach (Passover), Feast of Matzah (Unleavened Bread), Bikurim (Feast of First Fruits), Shavuot (Pentecost), Rosh Hashana (Feast of Trumpets), Yom Kippur (Day of Atonement), and Sukkot (Feast of Tabernacles). I would like to give you just a taste of what I have learned from these feasts and how important they were to Yeshua.

As I write this, we have just celebrated the Feast of Passover. It was a delightful evening of going through the Seder (Order) Service with a family of five. The children delighted in the participation. We followed a Messianic version of the Haggadah (telling) of the story of the Exodus from Egypt and how the Passover Seder reveals the Messiah in an amazing way. We saw how Yeshua took the middle matzah from the three-pouch matzah bag and broke it as He said, "*This is my body, which is broken for you.*"[8] We were amazed as we realized the pouch contained three matzah. Jewish traditions have differing opinions regarding what the three matzah stand for. Some even consider them to represent the Father, Word, and Spirit. We saw the bruises and stripes on the matzah representing how Yeshua was crucified. We washed each other's feet and blessed each other, remembering that Yeshua washed His disciple's feet.

We remembered the way He delivered all of us out of bondage to sin and became the Lamb, who was slain for us. We recounted our own testimonies and shared tears as we remembered His suffering and shame when we ate the "bitter herbs" (horseradish). We were reminded that He took the third cup, after supper, which represents the "cup of redemption." Yeshua said, "*This cup is the New Covenant, ratified by my blood, which is being poured out for you.*"[9]

We did all of this in remembrance of Him. Then we sang songs of Praise from the Hallel (Psalms 113-118) and rejoiced in our Salvation (Yeshua). Our bellies were full, our spirits were overflowing, and we rested in His joy.

The day before, we "housecleaned" the house and vacuumed all the cupboards because it says, "*on the first day remove the leaven from your houses.*" The command is given in Exodus 12:15. The Feast of Unleavened Bread is a whole week of becoming very aware of the role of leaven in our lives. Leaven (Hametz) is basically "yeast" and, in a Biblical sense, represents sin. Just as we go through the house and remove yeast and yeast products and crumbs, we need to examine our hearts for the leaven of sin. This is why the Apostle Sha'ul (Paul) said:

> **Get rid of the old hametz, so that you can be a new batch of dough, because in reality you are unleavened. For our Pesach lamb, the Messiah, has been sacrificed. So let us celebrate the Seder not with leftover hametz, the hametz of wickedness and evil, but with the matzah of purity and truth.**
> **(I Corinthians 5:7-8)**

Did you know that the Apostles celebrated all the Feasts of YHVH and kept the Sabbath? It wasn't until much later in history that these Feasts were eliminated by the church. We will get to that later.

I love the Feast of Unleavened Bread because it is always good to examine oneself and become aware of the reason YHVH asked us to do certain things. It is the origin of "spring cleaning." Yeshua was spotless, without sin, and His death ushered in this Feast.

The Feast of First Fruits has been one that can be interpreted in various ways concerning when it begins. It is clear that it starts the counting of the Omar, the fifty day count to Shavuot (Pentecost), but when this count begins has been the source of controversy.

The Bible indicates that it is the first day after the Shabbat following Passover. However, Passover is also considered a "Shabbat." So, in the Rabbinical calendar of this age, the counting of the Omer (the fifty days) begins the day after Passover.

However, according to Leviticus 23:15 there needs to be seven Shabbats observed in the counting. It would seem to me, that it should be the first day of the week following Passover. The reason I believe this, is because Yeshua rose from the dead on the Feast of First Fruits to fulfill its purpose. If He rose on the *"first day of the week"* (Matthew 28:1), it could be any time from sundown ending the Shabbat (Saturday), until the morning of the first day of the week (Sunday).

The women went to the tomb in the morning. He was already gone by then. If He was crucified on Passover and spent "three days and three nights" in the grave, then it could not be that the Feast of First Fruits was on the day after Passover that year. Calculating the forty days until His ascension and ten more days until Shavuot, it makes sense to begin the count on the first day of the week. Actually, many Messianic Jewish congregations follow this rule.

I am ashamed to say that until recently, I never knew that "Pentecost" was a Biblical Feast of the Lord! I only knew it in the Christian church as the day the Holy Spirit was poured out on the believers after Yeshua ascended into heaven. I was told it was the "birth of the church." I am so glad YHVH set me straight and taught me that there is so much more! I had missed so much!

Shavuot – fifty days after the Feast of First Fruits is also called a Bikurim (First Fruits) because first fruits of the harvest were presented at this time. It was one of the three feasts when YHVH required all men to *"appear at the place where I choose to place My Name"* (Deuteronomy 16:16). There are so many details of both of these Feasts relating to the barley and wheat harvests that play into the depths of what YHVH was accomplishing in His Plan through Yeshua. It is believed that the giving of the Torah at Mt. Sinai was timed with this Feast. Many will spend the night before Shavuot praying and studying Torah. The most important reason why YHVH chose this day to pour out His Spirit on the believers in Jerusalem, is because Truth and Spirit are partners. You can't have one without the other. Truth was given on Shavuot in the wilderness to Israel on physical tablets as law. The Spirit was given on Shavuot to the followers of Yeshua fulfilling the prophetic promise:

> **I will give you a new heart and put a new spirit inside you; I will take the stony heart out of your flesh and give you a heart of flesh. I will put my Spirit inside you and cause you to live by my laws, respect my rulings and obey them.** (Ezekiel 36:26-27)

Jewish people use the term "given," not "received," for the Torah. It is an ongoing process of receiving YHVH's instructions. So, also the Spirit was "given," meaning it was not just a once and done thing. It is an ongoing receiving that we open ourselves up to. More and more of Him! *"More Love. More Power. More of You in My Life."* [10]

This outpouring of the Spirit on the believers had the purpose of them receiving the power and instruction needed to spread the Good News of Yeshua, to be His hands and feet to the ends of the Earth! Without that power and infilling, the revelation of Yeshua would have remained with the disciples and believers of that day. YHVH was making His spirit available to "all who believe." He was going to fulfill His desire to spread His message to the Gentiles, too. The believers were given "tongues" of fire. They spoke in the languages of the people present at the Feast. This was a sign that we could be given gifts to be able to reach all people (Acts 2).

✡ ✡ ✡ ✡ ✡

Looking forward to the Fall Feasts, we have Rosh Hashana (Feast of Trumpets – Shofars) marking the beginning of the Civil New Year. Shofars are blown to usher in the Ten Days of Awe between Rosh Hashana and Yom Kippur (The Day of Atonement). There is not much given to us from the TaNaKH regarding Rosh Hashana. It is simply a day of blowing the shofars and proclaiming the new year. However, there is a clue in the Psalms.

How happy are the people who know the joyful shout!
They walk in the light of your presence, ADONAI.
(Psalm 89:16(15)) [11]

The words "the joyful shout" in Hebrew is "teruah" which is the sound of the Shofar! So, according to this verse, we are blessed when we hear the sound of the Shofar and we walk in the light of Adonai's presence! I want to do that, don't you? Perhaps this Feast is the day we will hear the "Shofar of YHVH" when He calls us to the Wedding Feast of Yeshua.

The most amazing thing about this Feast to be fulfilled in the future is how much it points to a wedding. The Bridegroom has been preparing a place for us and will come for us. Traditionally, a Jewish man will come for his bride at a day or hour that the bride does not know exactly. She must be ready at all times! She will know that it is within a 24 to 48 hour window, but she will not be certain of the exact time. So, she has her bridal gown ready and has been preparing herself during the season of betrothal. All of a sudden she hears the sound of the shofar. The Bridegroom is coming!! Her heart races as she thinks of what it will be like to see him again. They have been separated for what seems like an eternity! Now he is coming for her and will make her his bride. She can hardly wait. She quickly dresses and goes out to meet him. He takes her in his arms and says "I have returned for you, my darling, my bride." They go to the wedding and "live happily ever after." Who says there are no love stories in the Bible? [12]

Yom Kippur is the Day of Atonement. It is the tenth day of the seventh month. We were in the Old City of Jerusalem in 2010 on this day. Ronald and I went to the Kotel (Wailing Wall) to pray. This is the only day in Israel when everything is quiet and still. No cars. Nothing open. A complete fast. We each went to our perspective sides of the wall to pray.

Afterward, we came together in the courtyard and lingered there. All of a sudden I gasped and said, "He's here!" I knew in my Spirit that Yeshua was among us. I did not physically see Him, but something in my Spirit knew. I felt He was showing me that He was walking among His people, touching hearts that were seeking YHVH and His Messiah and would be open to receiving Him that year. I was profoundly moved. As we shared, both Ronald and I had specifically prayed that Yeshua would come "visit" His people.

Although I believe Yeshua became the perfect Atonement for our sins and completed His sacrifice so that we no longer need atonement, it is a good time to remind us to pray and seek YHVH and search our own hearts for things we may need to repent of and to intercede for His people. [13]

The final Feast is Sukkot (The Feast of Tabernacles). This is an eight day Feast full of celebration. Biblically, we are to remember our years in the wilderness and celebrate them by living in "booths" or "sukkot," which are elaborately decorated. It is believed that the American Thanksgiving was originally inspired by Sukkot. There are many similarities. Many believe this Feast will be fulfilled by the Millennium or thousand year reign of Messiah on earth.

If you have not experienced the Feasts of YHVH, may I encourage you to do so? Getting a taste of the Divine Appointments in the Feasts of YHVH will fill you with such delight that you will never have the need to observe any other holiday! The whole year is full of preparation and celebration. If you have a family with children or grandchildren, these feasts are a wonderful way to teach them the Scriptures! There is always something YHVH included for the little ones and these feasts are no exception. Perhaps that is why Yeshua said we had to "become as a child" to enter the Kingdom of Heaven!

Did you know that YHVH likes a party? He also loves good food. You think Thanksgiving is great? Just think about seven of them! Actually there are seventy plus! Every Sabbath is a Thanksgiving and the other seven Feasts are added in. Include the New Moon every month and special days, such as Hanukah and Purim, and before you know it the year is beginning over again with Passover. *"Oh the depths of the riches and the wisdom and knowledge of God!"* (Romans11:33) See what "Christians" have missed all these years?

We have some dear friends who live in a community in Judea. They were actually one of the four founding families of this town back in the 70's long before the word "settlement" became a bad political and media blitz against Israel. Now there are over 2000 inhabitants of which over 1200 are children. Talk about being fruitful and multiplying! Quite frequently we receive emails from them telling us of all the celebrations in their community. There are Bar Mitzvahs and B'rit Milah celebrations, all the holidays, and anniversaries—a never ending flow of celebration in the Name of YHVH. We applaud their Biblical lifestyle and the example they are giving their fellow Jewish people that believing in YHVH's promises to Israel brings forth great fruit.

Christians have lost the depths of the riches of what YHVH had set up as Divine Appointments with Him. Yeshua fulfilled everything on a Feast day. He died on Passover, rose from the dead on the Feast of First Fruits, poured out His Spirit on Shavuot, and will come again during the Fall feasts, perhaps the Feast of Trumpets. Did you know that in the Millennium we will celebrate not only the Sabbath and New Moon festivals, but the Feast of Tabernacles (Sukkot)?

Finally, everyone remaining from all the nations that came to attack Yerushalayim will go up every year to worship the king, ADONAI-Tzva'ot, and to keep the festival of Sukkot. If any of the families of the earth does not go up to Yerushalayim to worship the king, ADONAI-Tzva'ot, no rain will fall on them. (Zechariah 14:16-17)

77

YHVH means business!

So why have we lost the name of Yeshua, the meaning of Hebrew word concepts, and the feasts? Do we need a history lesson? I don't like this history lesson, but if we are going to be good archeologists, we need to keep digging until we really reach the very depths of the bottom of our souls and expose the foundation stone. Are you willing to go there with me? Put on your "muck" boots, we're going to be getting into the muddy section of our excavation!

----

[1] A very interesting study of the Hebrew calendar, scientifically and Biblically is the Torah Calendar. The following link gives a detailed description of determining the Hebrew year. The site also gives the determination of months and other interesting topics: http://www.torahcalendar.com/ORBITS.asp?HebrewDay=15&HebrewMonth=1&Year=2013
A basic overview of the Hebrew calendar can be found at: http://en.wikipedia.org/wiki/Hebrew_calendar

[2] Many countries in the western Asian region used the Mesopotamian calendar from very early times, though the names of months varied. Prior to the Babylonian exile, the names of only four months are referred to in the Tanakh: Aviv - first month - literally "spring" (Exodus 12:2, 13:4, 23:15, 34:18, Deut. 16:1); Ziv - second month - literally "light" (1Kings 6:1 6:37); Ethanim - seventh month - literally "strong" in plural, perhaps referring to strong rains (1Kings 8:2); and Bul - eighth month (1Kings 6:38). All of these are believed to be Canaanite names, and at least two are Phoenician (Northern Canaanite). During the Babylonian exile, which started in 586 BCE, Babylonian month names were adopted, which are still in use. http://en.wikipedia.org/wiki/Hebrew_calendarhttp://www.angelfire.com/pa2/passover/months-of-the-jewish-calendar.html

[3] Jonathan Cahn, *The Harbinger: The Ancient Mystery That Holds the Secret of America's Future,* Charisma Media/Charisma House Book Group, Lake Mary, Florida, 2012. See also his website for other reference materials : http://www.bethisraelworshipcenter.org/Index.htm

[4] Genesis 2:3

[5]The English names for the days of the week have a mixed origin, some being named for the Sun and Moon, and others being named for Roman, Nordic, or Germanic gods and goddesses (these being introduced to the British Isles by invaders from the Continent.) Sunday is named for the sun. Monday is named for the moon. Tuesday is named for Tiu, Tyr, or Tiwa, who was a Germanic god. Wednesday is named for Woden, Odin, or Wotan which are the names of a Nordic/Germanic god. Thursday is named for Thor, Donar, or Thunor, also a Nordic/Germanic god. Friday is named for Frigg or Freia who was a Nordic goddess. Saturday is named for Saturn, who was a Roman god. http://wiki.answers.com/Q/How_did_the_days_of_the_week_get_their_names

[6] Strong's H7676 from H7637

[7] Strong's H4150

[8] Luke 22:19

[9] Luke 22:20

[10] Words of a worship song by Jude del Hierro

[11] The Hebrew Tanakh (Old Testament) uses a different numbering for the verses in Psalms and some of the Prophets' books – hence the second number in the parentheses (#).

[12] A beautiful portrayal of a Biblical betrothal is depicted in the documentary called *Betrothed, the Story of Brandon and Tali Waller*, Third Dawn LLC, 2010, thirdawn.com or hayovel.org

[13] I recommend a book by Rabbi Jim Appel, *Yom Teruah" The Day of Sounding the Shofar, Appointed Times Series – Rosh Hashanah*, Olive Press Messianic and Christian Publisher, Copenhagen, NY, 2012. Rabbi Jim gives wonderful detail of this Feast as well as the Ten Days of Awe leading up to Yom Kippur. For those of us who know very little, the depths of our Messianic brothers and sisters fills in the gaps! *"...if Isra'el's being placed temporarily in a condition less favored than that of the Gentiles is bringing riches to the latter — how much greater riches will Israel in its fullness bring them!"* (Romans 11:12).

9

The Ancient Paths

Here is what ADONAI says: "Stand at the crossroads
and look; ask about the ancient paths, 'Which one
is the good way?' Take it, and you will find rest for
your souls." But they said, "We will not take it." I
appointed sentinels to direct them: "Listen for the
sound of the shofar." But they said, "We will not
listen." (Jeremiah 6:16)

Enter through the narrow gate; for the gate is wide
and the way is broad that leads to destruction, and
there are many who enter through it. For the gate is
small and the way is narrow that leads to life, and
there are few who find it. (Matthew 7:13-14 NASB)

Yeshua said, "I AM the Way -- and the Truth and
the Life; no one comes to the Father except through
me." (John 14:6)

I had a dream one night several years ago. In the dream
I saw a translucent globe that seemed to represent "heaven." In
the globe was the "Ancient of Days" sitting on a throne glowing
in light. His hair was pure white and He was laughing and
rejoicing over gifts He was receiving. As He would unwrap a
gift, He would lift a person out of the box and give them a big
hug. They then would join a whole group of others praising
Him with their arms raised. They were all wearing white robes.

As I looked further in my dream I saw earth. In the center of the earth Yeshua was standing. In front of Him were all manner of people from every race and age standing in a line. As one person would approach Yeshua, they would bow on their knees before Him. He would lift them up and embrace them. Then He would wrap them up in a package and send them up to heaven via a conveyor belt that looked like a human blood vein! (Although I didn't see it, I imagine He clothed them in the white robe, or that happened as they were ascending.)

I realized through my dream that I was being shown what redemption really meant. The blood vein was Yeshua's atoning sacrifice. Sin had separated us from the Father and now, through Yeshua, we can come to Him. But more importantly is how thrilled the Father is to receive us! We are gifts to Him. He doesn't want to be separated from His creation. He desires us all to be wrapped up in a package and brought to worship before Him. I saw the immense joy in both Yeshua and the Father. I remember continuing my dream by running to my sister and saying, "I finally get it! I finally get it!"

In an earlier chapter we established how the name Yeshua became Jesus. Then we looked at several words, whose depths of meaning have been lost in translation. Finally, we looked at the Sabbath and the Feasts of YHVH. The question continues "What does it matter?" Let's do some more digging into our archeological site and see what else we discover. Be patient, I will give my response, for I have been asking that question for a very long time. Try not to jump ahead to the "who done it?" page. We still have a long way to go, down some ancient paths.

Although Ronald and I never went to Israel as typical "tourists" or with a tour group, during one of our visits we went on a tour of the City of David (Ir David), which is outside the current "Old City" walls of Jerusalem, to the south.

Jerusalem has been taken over 35 times in its history and is the most hotly contested piece of real estate in the world! This particular part of Jerusalem is where one may hear of rock throwing and car bombings because it is also a predominantly Arab Muslim area in what is known as Silwan, in "East Jerusalem." This would be where King David conquered the Jebusites when he began his reign in Jerusalem. (See II Samuel 5.)

When Israel regained this area in 1967, they began to excavate what they believed to be the original foundation stones of Jerusalem. The importance of this excavation site and National Park cannot be underestimated. Here the very foundation stones of the City of Jerusalem and the Biblical history of the Jewish people come alive. Truth is being exposed daily. Our tour guide used only one thing as her reference – a TaNaKH Bible. She read Scriptures that pointed to where we were standing at the moment and told us what was traditionally thought to be the location. Then she would tell us why the traditional view was incorrect. Where once they thought the Pool of Siloam was has been usurped by the actual location, which was found when a water main burst and the street had to be dug up!

They are exposing, not only the foundation stones of ancient Jerusalem, but they are correcting history! It is the most amazing experience. I felt like I was in a time warp. Quite frequently we receive updates from the Ir David Foundation[1] which share new things that have been discovered and exposed under the layers of rubble. I have never felt so close to the heart of YHVH than in that spot and I get extremely excited about this place!

When David wrote the Psalms, he wrote them from there. As you enter the Ir David park, there is a tower alongside the place where they believe King David's palace stood. One can ascend the steps to the top of the tower and view the surrounding area. The perspective from that particular place reveals the mountains that surround Jerusalem (Psalm 125). From the Temple Mount (Mt. Zion), the Mount of Olives, The Mount of Offence, The Mount of Evil Council, and the Western Hill, as you look down into the depths of the Kidron Valley, you feel the importance of this "stronghold" that was taken by David and became Israel's capital. In addition, Psalm 48 verse 3(2)[2] makes no sense unless you are standing in the City of David. Mount Zion is only to the north in this location. (The photo on the back cover of this book is from part of this site.)

There are many other archeological parks around Israel that are exposing Biblical History. Much is yet to be discovered and pieces of the puzzle put together, but we are finding the fragments that affirm and confirm the truths of the Bible. It is exciting to be a part of this age of uncovering.

By being willing to dig through the rubble of thousands of years, archeologists are revealing the truth! If tradition was incorrect, they are able to correct it. If not, they affirm it. If they are willing to do this with physical dirt, should we not be digging deeper into our own Bibles and its history to discover truth? Should we not be willing to have been wrong about something we came to believe as truth for so long because "it's always been that way" (tradition)? We must be willing to ask ourselves the hard questions.

The New Covenant book of Acts is a wonderful historical account of the "move of the spirit" in the days following Yeshua's death and resurrection. We explored the calendar of YHVH for these appointed times in the last chapter, but now, let's see what happened to the followers of what was known as "The Way."

In Acts chapter 9 we find the account of Sha'ul (Saul) who is breathing "murderous threats" against the disciples of Yeshua. It is documented in verse 2 that he asked for letters from the high priest authorizing him to *"arrest any people he might find, whether men or women, who belonged to 'the Way' and bring them back to Jerusalem."*

Although the Jewish people were looking for a Messiah, Yeshua didn't seem to fit their idea of what the Messiah would be like because he didn't conquer the Romans and did not start a political revolution. What they seemed to miss is the fact that Yeshua did start a revolution. He started a spiritual one! He had said, *"My kingdom is not of this world"* (John 18:36), but it wasn't understood. There are many Jewish people today who still do not believe there is any way that Yeshua is the Messiah because he did not fulfill certain major prophesies that the Messiah was to fulfill.[3]

When we were in Israel in 2010, we noticed flyers plastered on many doors in Jerusalem announcing that Menacham Schneerson is the Messiah. I wanted to find out who this man was and why his followers would deem him the Messiah. He was indeed a very great Rabbi and did much to further Jewish education around the world. He was born in Nikolaev, Russia (present-day Mykolaiv, Ukraine). He died at the age of 92 in Brooklyn, New York, honored and revered.[4] Even though he has not "risen" from the dead, he is still considered the Messiah by many of his Chabad Lubavich followers.[5]

I find it very interesting that all of Menacham Schneerson's followers are still considered Jewish, while Jewish followers of Yeshua are not. My thought as I was reading Schneerson's history, as well as a book against "missionaries,"[6] was that no matter who anyone thinks the Messiah is or should be, there is only one thing that will verify his authenticity. That is the Resurrection. Every possible Messiah in the future will be human and will have to die. Why was it so hard to believe that Yeshua must die? He had to die. It was the only way He could redeem us! There was no other way. If He didn't die for the very reason He did, He would not have been the Messiah! He had to be persecuted. He had to be left alone. He had to come as the "suffering servant" of Isaiah 53 and lay His life down. He could not be like us! He had to be "other."

The only proof of His being truly Messiah was that He had to conquer the very thing that sin caused us all to do - die. Then He had to be resurrected. Death could not hold Him. He had to conquer it. He is the only one of those forty supposed "messiahs" that did. The rest are in their graves. So, when He rose from the dead, why didn't He stick around and do the conquering at that time? Why did He leave us? Ah, that is the million dollar question. He gave us the answer.

"But I tell you the truth, it is to your advantage that I go away; <u>for if I don't go away, the comforting Counselor will not come to you.</u> However, if I do go, I will send him to you. When he comes, <u>he will show that the world is wrong about sin, about righteousness and about judgment</u>, about sin, in that <u>people don't put their trust in me</u>; about righteousness, in that I am going to the Father and you will no longer see me; about judgment, in that the ruler of this world has been judged. I still have many things to tell you, but you can't bear them now. However, <u>when the Spirit of Truth comes, he will guide you into all the truth;</u> for he will not speak on his own initiative but will say only what he hears. He will also announce to you the events of the future. He will glorify me, because he will receive from what is mine and announce it to you." (John 16:7-14)

The Torah of Truth is given at Mt. Sinai. The Spirit of Truth is given in Jerusalem at the Feast of Shavuot following Yeshua's death, resurrection, and ascension. Both being given at the appointed time of YHVH.[7] Yeshua is telling us that He is sending, from the Father, a move of the Ruach HaKodesh (Holy Spirit) that has never been seen before.[8] This "Spirit of Truth" would be an extension of Himself, meaning He would be with(in) us spiritually, and would teach us all truth. After His resurrection, Yeshua spent time with His disciples, giving them instructions and helping them understand YHVH's plan. He had already "breathed" on them and said, *"Receive the Holy Spirit"* (John 20:22). He also told them:

> **"This is what I meant when I was still with you and told you that everything written about me in the Torah of Moshe, the Prophets and the Psalms had to be fulfilled." Then he opened their minds, so that they could understand the Tanakh, telling them, "Here is what it says: the Messiah is to suffer and to rise from the dead on the third day; and in his name repentance leading to forgiveness of sins is to be proclaimed to people from all nations, starting with Yerushalayim. You are witnesses of these things. Now I am sending forth upon you what my Father promised, so stay here in the city until you have been equipped with power from above." (Luke 24:44-48)**

It would be the power through which the disciples and followers of Yeshua would have the courage to continue on in spite of persecution. It would be the source of their message, their strength, their giftings, and their ministry. As followers of Yeshua, we would become His hands and feet, and like Him, fulfill the Isaiah prophecy, empowered and anointed:

> **The Spirit of Adonai Elohim is upon me, because Adonai has anointed me to announce good news to the poor. He has sent me to heal the brokenhearted; to proclaim freedom to the captives, to let out into**

light those bound in the dark; to proclaim the year of the favor of Adonai and the day of vengeance of our God; to comfort all who mourn, yes, provide for those in Tziyon who mourn, giving them garlands instead of ashes, the oil of gladness instead of mourning, a cloak of praise instead of a heavy spirit, so that they will be called oaks of righteousness planted by Adonai in which he takes pride. (Isaiah 61:1-3)

I know there is more. I long to understand the depths of the Spirit. I will continue seeking YHVH for more revelation— more depth. To be continued......

In the meantime..... Let's get back to history.

The followers of Yeshua, after His resurrection and ascension, were called "the Way" and were considered a sect of Judaism. There were over 5,000 Jewish believers in Yeshua in the early days of the book of Acts. As we mentioned earlier, Sha'ul (Saul) is so convinced that they are wrong about Yeshua, that he becomes a vigilante and begins to hunt down Yeshua's followers, convinced he is doing the will of God. He is one that is standing by when Stephen is stoned in Acts 7. Persecution has begun. Of course Sha'ul (now Paul) has a dramatic encounter with Yeshua himself and he is completely transformed and joins the "sect" of followers. It is amazing what an encounter with Yeshua will do. May we all have such a privilege![9]

In the meantime, the Spirit of YHVH is beginning to broaden these follower's views of who Yeshua was sent to "save." Yes, He was sent to "save His people from their sins," but YHVH has so much more intended. He wants the whole world to hear the Gospel—Good News—of Yeshua. He has in mind that everyone should know and come "into the

Kingdom." There were many Scriptures that pointed to this, but it was hard for the Jewish followers of Yeshua to get it. It took the "Spirit of Truth" to reveal it to them.

In fact, it took a vision and a visitation for the first disciples to "get it." We see this story in Acts 10. Kefa (Peter) saw a vision of a large sheet being lowered to the ground with all kinds of creatures in it. Some were clean and some were unclean. A voice said, *"Get up, slaughter, and eat!"* Kefa was appalled. He had never broken the command of the Torah regarding unclean animals and he had never eaten in the house of a "Goy" (Gentile). The voice told him to *"stop treating as unclean what God has made clean."* This happened to him three times! Kefa was still puzzling over this when some men came to the door asking for him to come and visit with a Gentile!

When he gets to the Gentile's home, he tells them, ***"You are well aware that for a man who is a Jew to have close association with someone who belongs to another people, or to come and visit him, is something that just isn't done. But God has shown me not to call any person common or unclean"*** (vs 28).

I'll bet you've been told that this verse means that it doesn't matter what you eat! Look again. It says that God showed him the purpose of the vision was to break open his view of *people*. He wanted them to start going to the Gentiles to spread the Good News of Yeshua!

The Ruach HaKodesh (Holy Spirit) falls on all the people who were there and they had not even been water baptized! Talk about an earthquake shift in a person's "tradition." Yochanan the Immerser (John the Baptist) had prophesied this event. ***It's true that I am immersing you in water so that you might turn from sin to God; but the one coming after me is more powerful than I—I'm not worthy even to carry his sandals—and he will immerse you in the Ruach HaKodesh and in fire*** (Matthew 3:11)

THE ANCIENT PATHS

I, Adonai, called you righteously, I took hold of you
by the hand, I shaped you and made you a covenant
for the people; to be a light for the Goyim (Gentiles),
so that you can open blind eyes, free the prisoners
from confinement, those living in darkness from the
dungeon. (Isaiah 42:6-7)

I believe it has always been YHVH's purpose for Israel
to affect the nations and to spread the news of His righteousness
to *all* peoples of the world. However, it never happened that
way because they became like the nations around them, instead
of the nations around them becoming like them! They were
to represent YHVH and become like Him. The whole purpose
of YHVH has always been to draw mankind to Himself to
dwell in His presence and become righteous. Moshe (Moses)
understood this:

"Now, please, if it is really the case that I have found
favor in your sight, show me your ways; so that I will
understand you and continue finding favor in your
sight. Moreover, keep on seeing this nation as your
people." He answered, "Set your mind at rest—my
presence will go with you, after all." Moshe replied,
"If your presence doesn't go with us, don't make us
go on from here. For how else is it to be known that
I have found favor in your sight, I and your people,
other than by your going with us? That is what
distinguishes us, me and your people, from all the
other peoples on earth." (Exodus 33:13-16)

We see in these verses the heart of the matter for Moshe
(Moses). It is all about the Presence of YHVH going with him/
them. He "gets" it that if YHVH doesn't go with them, nothing
else matters. These verses also affirm that His people were to

89

be "distinguished" from other people on the earth. We have never gotten the message. Israel didn't get it and we don't get it. "Few find it," Yeshua said. It's all about Him, not about us. When YHVH sanctified His people (Israel), He chose them to be a "set apart" people—distinguished.

There were many things they were not to do, but it was because they were not to *"do what is done in the land of Egypt"* (Leviticus 18:3 NASB). In other words, they were not to learn the ways of the nations, because He knew it would just lure them away. He wanted a "holy" nation, a "royal" priesthood, righteousness and order. They were not to set up kings and were not to be like the nations.

However, as the Bible shows us, it didn't happen that way. No more had they set up their homes in the Promised Land, then they were being oppressed by one group after another because they did not obey YHVH's orders. It was all for their own good to bring them back to YHVH!

I have to ask—what is different about now? What distinguishes *us* from the rest of the world? If I look at most "Christian" churches, I see more of the world than Yeshua. I see people "playing" church and playing games and not taking YHVH or Yeshua very seriously at all. We now have cafes in our churches. You can come on a Sunday morning and drink a cup of Java and have a sweet roll before going in to be entertained by a band and a speaker! Another danger I see in the church is their interest in "other religions" and the study of things like the Koran or Eastern Religions. From personal experience, it is very dangerous to study other religions. YHVH knew that it could lure us to accept them or even desire to know or experience more. I have seen in my own life that studying other religions drew me away from the faith; it did not keep me true.

A.W. Tozer, in his book, *Divine Conquest* says, *"The world is whitewashed just enough to pass inspection by blind men posing as believers and those believers are everlastingly seeking to gain acceptance with the world.....The world's spirit is strong and it clings to us.....It can change its face to suit any circumstance and so deceive many a simple Christian whose senses are not exercised to discern good from evil.....Both the sons of this world and the sons of God have been baptized into a spirit- but the spirit of the world and the Spirit that dwells in the hearts of twice born men are as far apart as heaven and hell.... The world...is simply unregenerate human nature, wherever it is found, whether in a tavern or a church."[10]*

Can we stretch this just a bit further without the rubber band breaking? I believe we have misquoted and misinterpreted the Apostle Sha'ul (Paul)'s letters. Our perspective has been of a Greek instead of a Hebrew mindset. We have also taken his writings as if they were written to churches in the last 1700 years instead of the era in which they were written, almost 2000 years ago.

I would like to introduce Sha'ul as a Jewish man in the first century who has an incredible heart for his people, the Jewish people. He is a Torah observant, Sabbath and Feast keeping Jew who strongly believes in preserving the essence of the Torah and the TaNaKH. (See Philippians 3.) What he is against is the perversion of Torah in legalistic religious observance, and he is against a "separatist" mentality which puts people in categories instead of freeing them to be all Yeshua meant them to be. He "gets" dying to self. He "gets" the purpose of Yeshua's life, death, and resurrection. He "gets" that the adversary is out to destroy what YHVH set up. He "gets" that we need the empowering transformation of the Holy Spirit or what we produce will be wood, hay, and stubble!

He is writing with only the TaNaKH Scriptures as a reference. He is writing *before* the council of Nicea and the Gentile "church fathers" were even born and the "religion" of

Christianity was created. He is coming from an assumption that there is a righteous, Godly way of doing things and a pagan, worldly way.

The Gentiles of his time were totally immersed in paganism and idolatrous pagan practices. He realizes the challenges Gentiles have in facing fellow Gentiles with their new faith in Yeshua. As a Jew, the Roman government would excuse the non-worship of their pagan gods, but as a Gentile, they were not excused.[11] Persecution was very severe and many Gentiles were tempted to go back to their former way of life. If we come to Sha'ul's teachings and letters with this perspective we can perhaps read the oft quoted passages with a different conclusion. He is talking to Gentile believers, not fellow Jews when he says:

> **In the past, when you did not know God, you served as slaves beings which in reality are non-gods. But now you do know God, and, more than that, you are known by God. So how is it that you turn back again to those weak and miserable elemental spirits? Do you want to enslave yourselves to them once more? You observe special days, months, seasons and years! (Galatians 4:8-10)**

Sha'ul is writing to the Galatians, most likely before Acts 15 (the first Jerusalem council ruling of what was permissible for the Gentiles). The special days, months, seasons, and years are pagan, not Jewish!

In Romans, Sha'ul really displays his heart for his people. He is begging us to understand their position and the fact that YHVH has not rejected them, but is waiting for a fulfillment of His Plan for both Jews and Gentiles. It is a far greater Plan than we could imagine and Sha'ul has only caught a "glimpse" of it. May I encourage you to read and study the book of Romans, specifically chapters 9-11? David Stern does an excellent job of translating this text from a Hebrew mindset. I never understood the book of Romans until I read it from the Hebrew perspective. Let's hear what Sha'ul is saying:

> Then what advantage has the Jew? What is the value of being circumcised? Much in every way! In the first place, the Jews were entrusted with the very words of God. If some of them were unfaithful, so what? Does their faithlessness cancel God's faithfulness? Heaven forbid! God would be true even if everyone were a liar! ... So are we Jews better off? Not entirely; for I have already made the charge that all people, Jews and Gentiles alike, are controlled by sin. As the Tanakh puts it "There is no one righteous, not even one! No one understands, no one seeks God, all have turned away; there is no one who shows kindness, not a single one!" (Romans 3: 1-4a,9-12)

> "In that case, I say, isn't it that God has repudiated his people?" Heaven forbid! For I myself am a son of Isra'el, from the seed of Avraham, of the tribe of Binyamin. God has not repudiated his people, whom he chose in advance. Or don't you know what the Tanakh says about Eliyahu? He pleads with God against Isra'el, "ADONAI, they have killed your prophets and torn down your altars, and I'm the only one left, and now they want to kill me too!" But what is God's answer to him? "I have kept for myself seven thousand men who have not knelt down to Ba'al." It's the same way in the present age: there is a remnant, chosen by grace. (Now if it is by grace, it is accordingly not based on legalistic works; if it were otherwise, grace would no longer be grace.) What follows is that Isra'el has not attained the

goal for which she is striving. The ones chosen have obtained it, but the rest have been made stonelike, just as the Tanakh says, "God has given them a spirit of dullness — eyes that do not see and ears that do not hear, right down to the present day." And David says, "Let their dining table become for them a snare and a trap, a pitfall and a punishment. Let their eyes be darkened, so that they can't see, with their backs bent continually." "In that case, I say, isn't it that they have stumbled with the result that they have permanently fallen away?" Heaven forbid! Quite the contrary, it is by means of their stumbling that the deliverance has come to the Gentiles, in order to provoke them to jealousy. Moreover, if their stumbling is bringing riches to the world - that is, if Isra'el's being placed temporarily in a condition less favored than that of the Gentiles is bringing riches to the latter — how much greater riches will Isra'el in its fullness bring them! ..... "But if some of the branches were broken off, and you — a wild olive — were grafted in among them and have become equal sharers in the rich root of the olive tree, then don't boast as if you were better than the branches! However, if you do boast, remember that you are not supporting the root, the root is supporting you. So you will say, "Branches were broken off so that I might be grafted in." True, but so what? They were broken off because of their lack of trust. However, you keep your place only because of your trust. So don't be arrogant; on the contrary, be terrified! For if God did not spare the natural branches, he certainly won't spare you! So take a good look at God's kindness and his severity: on the one hand, severity toward those who fell off; but, on the other hand, God's kindness

toward you — provided you maintain yourself in
that kindness! Otherwise, you too will be cut off!"
(Romans 11:1-12,17-22)

What was YHVH's Plan for the new believers? What
is YHVH's vision of the One New Man? Where does Torah
come in? Let us consider these passages:

Never lie to one another; because you have stripped
away the old self, with its ways, and have put on
the new self, which is continually being renewed
in fuller and fuller knowledge, closer and closer to
the image of its Creator. The new self allows no
room for discriminating between Gentile and Jew,
circumcised and uncircumcised, foreigner, savage,
slave, free man; on the contrary, in all, the Messiah
is everything. (Colosians 3:9-11)

Therefore, remember your former state: you Gentiles
by birth—called the Uncircumcised by those who,
merely because of an operation on their flesh, are
called the Circumcised—at that time had no Messiah.
You were estranged from the national life of Isra'el.
You were foreigners to the covenants embodying
God's promise. You were in this world without hope
and without God. But now, you who were once far
off have been brought near through the shedding of
the Messiah's blood. For he himself is our shalom
- he has made us both one and has broken down
the m'chitzah which divided us by destroying in his
own body the enmity occasioned by the Torah, with
its commands set forth in the form of ordinances.
He did this in order to create in union with himself

from the two groups a single new humanity and thus make shalom, and in order to reconcile to God both in a single body by being executed on a stake as a criminal and thus in himself killing that enmity. Also, when he came, he announced as Good News shalom to you far off and shalom to those nearby, news that through him we both have access in one Spirit to the Father. So then, you are no longer foreigners and strangers. On the contrary, you are fellow-citizens with God's people and members of God's family. You have been built on the foundation of the emissaries and the prophets, with the cornerstone being Yeshua the Messiah himself. In union with him the whole building is held together, and it is growing into a holy temple in union with the Lord. Yes, in union with him, you yourselves are being built together into a spiritual dwelling-place for God! (Ephesians 2:11-22)

The promise of the New Covenant, as foretold by the prophets is for the goal of One New Man, a dwelling place for YHVH. The wilderness Tabernacle is the picture, example, and "shadow." Yeshua broke down the dividing wall of the separation between the Holy Place and the Holy of Holies. Now we can dwell in His presence through the Ruach HaKodesh (Holy Spirit). The goal is – one mind, one heart, one shepherd. Can you see why the adversary would try so hard to create religions so that we get side tracked and bogged down? Do you see why he tries so hard to bring division and continue the hatred toward YHVH's chosen people? Why are we feeding the adversary's plan and not the Plan of YHVH?

Ok. I'll get off my "soap box." I admit I got a "little" sidetracked. Maybe a lot. Please hang in there with me. You will see how this relates to history.

Things changed dramatically for the followers of the "Way." Toward 70 CE the Romans were about to "sack" Jerusalem. The followers of Yeshua felt they should follow His warning from Matthew 24:15-21 and *"flee to the hills"* when they saw Jerusalem surrounded. They did, and fled to Pella, which would now be in Jordan. After the destruction of the Temple and razing of Jerusalem, things for all of Judaism were turned upside down. By this time the whole of the book of Acts has transpired. The original apostles had been scattered and some had been killed. The Gentile believers had begun to really come to the knowledge of the Gospel of Yeshua in droves and as Sha'ul and Bar Nabba and others continued on their "missionary" journeys, they spread the Gospel far and wide. Sha'ul (Paul) was arrested and sent to Rome. (Read the account in the book of Acts. It is a "page turner!") By this time, he is probably dead as well. The only book left to be written is the Revelation of Yeshua as given to Yochanan (John). It is believed to have been written about 90-100 CE. He would have been an old man by then and in exile on the isle of Patmos during a severe persecution of believers.

Following this, a Jewish revolt was begun by a certain "Simon Bar Kochba." He was looked to as a "real" Messiah and had many followers. One of the great Rabbis of the day "Rabbi Akiva" supported Bar Kochba and deemed him the Messiah. Of course the followers of Yeshua would not join in this movement and so they were persecuted even more.

With all of the upheavals of government and nations, a good bit of history from this period is obscure. Some have done amazing work to try to recover what became of the Jewish believers in Yeshua.[12] By the end of the book of Acts there would have been tens of thousands of them. Some stayed in sects that were known as "Nazarenes." Some went off on tangents and diverted from the true Gospel and were known as "Ebionites."

In any case, two distinct things happened. One is that the sect of Jewish believers in Yeshua are now cast out of Judaism and deemed to be a part of the new "Christian" religion. The Jewish religious leaders have been relocated to Tiberius and have become stricter in their religious beliefs and practices. Rabbinic Judaism becomes the "New Religion" of the Jews which gives the Oral Law and writings of the Rabbis equal the sanctity to the Torah and Writings of the TaNaKH.[13]

At the same time, the Gentiles begin to develop their own version of a religion. They have already been pagans and they are now told they don't need to follow Torah, so they abandon it. They become haters of the Jews because of what they "did to Christ" and now the Jews are "Iesous" killers. Everything has been transferred to Greek and so the "New Religion" of the Gentiles becomes "Greek Christianity" and Yeshua becomes Greek too![14]

By 332, a Roman Emperor, Constantine deems Christianity the new government and forms his own non Jewish council, who decide what is in and what is out and who is in and who is out. The Jews are out. They will have nothing to do with them and they don't want any "Jewish" flavor in their "new" religion. If you read the vitriol of the early "church fathers," you will be appalled and, hopefully, ashamed. It should make you righteously angry! I won't give them the "time of day" here because I do not believe they deserve it. I will only say that it is readily available in books and on the internet.

I really like what my friend Rusty Richards said one time. *"When Christianity came to the Greeks they made it a philosophy. When it came to the Romans, it became a government. When it came to the Europeans, they made it a culture, and when it came to America, it became a business!"*[15] (I would add that in America it became a psychology, too!)

It looks like we've built our house on a pretty good pile of sand. Let's look next at who I believe YHVH's role model is for us as Gentile believers in Yeshua.

----
[1] Ir David Foundation (City of David) www.cityofdavid.org.il

[2] The Hebrew Tanakh (Old Testament) uses a different numbering for the verses in Psalms and some of the Prophets' books – hence the second number in the parentheses (#).

[3] Aryeh Kaplan, *The Real Messiah? A Jewish Response to Missionaries*, National Conference of Synagogue Youth, NY, NY, 1976, fourth printing 1995, pg 51-61.

[4] http://en.wikipedia.org/wiki/Menachem_Mendel_Schneerson#.22Moshia ch.22_.28Messiah.29_fervor

[5] Did you know that there are possibly forty persons who have claimed to be the Messiah or were thought to be the Messiah over the course of history? The first was in 4 BCE and the most recent is still living in Tel Aviv.

[6] Kaplan, *The Real Messiah,* pg 81-97.

[7] I give credit to my dear friend Patrina Ashley for this insight. I appreciate all of her insights and there are more that have infiltrated this book. Thank you for being you, Patrina!

[8] This would be a fulfillment of Yo'el 3:1 (Joel 2:28).

[9] One of the many miraculous modern day encounters with Yeshua is documented in Rabbi Greg Hershberg's book, *From the Projects to the Palace.* Published by Olive Press Messianic and Christian Publisher, it can be found on Amazon or by going to www.olivepresspublisher.com

[10] A.W. Tozer, *Divine Conquest,* published in Mass Market Press by Living Books, 1995. Mr. Tozer lived from 1897 – 1963 and wrote prolifically, challenging the Christian church in many areas.

[11] *First Fruits of Zion* CD set called "What about Paganism" by Toby Janicki, CD #2 www.ffoz.org

[12] Several authors have done a great scholarly job of bringing this portion of history to light. Here are a few:

Dr. Ron Moseley, *Yeshua: A guide to the Real Jesus and the Original Church,* Messianic Jewish Publishers, Clarkesville, MD, 1998.

Roy A Pritz, *Nazarene Jewish Christianity,* The Hebrew University Magnes Press, 1988.

Dan Juster, *Jewish Roots: A Foundation of Biblical Theology,* Destiny Image Publishers, Inc., Shippensburg, PA, 1995.

David A Stern, *Restoring the Jewishness of the Gospel,* Jewish New Testament Publisher, Clarkesville, MD, 1988, 1990, 2009.

[13] The Pharisees, after the fall of Jerusalem reorganize in Tiberias and in CE 90 they had the Council of Jamnia which condemned the "Nazarenes" sect as heretical. They also affirmed the standards of Orthodox Judaism. See Dan Juster, *Jewish Roots,* pg 139.

[14] Nehemia Gordon, *The Hebrew Yeshua vs the Greek Jesus,* Hilkiah Press, 2005, www.hilkiahpress.com

[15] Rusty and Janet Richards have been life long friends and have a wonderful ministry called "Pray Big." Their work in Europe and America has a similar calling: excavating, rebuilding, restoring, repairing. I bless them and their ministry! http://rustyandjanet.wordpress.com/

10

Ancient Role Model

"Don't press me to leave you and stop following you; for wherever you go, I will go; and wherever you stay, I will stay. Your people will be my people and your God will be my God. Where you die, I will die; and there I will be buried" (Ruth 1:16)

One of the books that deeply impacted my life during my own "excavation" days was *Your People Shall Be My People* by Don Finto. Don is an older, wise man of YHVH who knows how to gently and kindly express the truth to Gentile Christians. In his book, Don exposes something about the history of Christianity that has connected with me. Don shares the story of Ruth from Moab, the daughter-in-law of Naomi. Don compares Ruth to Gentile Christians.

> *I have come to see the believers from the nations foreshadowed in Ruth, who was the non-Jewish great-grandmother of King David. Though she did not come from the seed of Judah, she came fully into the heritage of Israel. Unlike the Church, however, Ruth did not bring her Gentile ways with her. She left her own people and covenanted herself to Naomi and later to Boaz. She committed to live and to die with Naomi and her people. I believe that should be the Gentile Church's stand with God's covenant family, whose promises we have entered.* [1] (Emphasis mine.)

There is so much more to this story. I'd like to dig a little deeper into it before we move on. I believe, like Pastor Finto, that non Jewish believers in Yeshua, are represented by Ruth (whose name means "friend"). In this story, Naomi becomes bitter because of the loss she has experienced. She believes the hand of YHVH has been against her. She lost her husband and both sons. She asks people to call her Marah, which means "bitter," instead of Naomi, which means "pleasant."

She is grieving her loss, but her daughter-in-law, a non-Jew, is actually instrumental to bringing blessing back into Naomi's life. Ruth goes out to glean the fields and YHVH directs her steps to Boaz' fields. Ruth doesn't know that he is a kinsman redeemer. She doesn't know the ways of the Jewish people. However, her servant heart does not go unnoticed and she is granted great favor through Boaz (whose name means "in him there is strength") and his workers. She has even caught the attention of the leaders of the city. Boaz tells her *"for all the city leaders among my people know that you are a woman of good character"* (3:11).

Boaz takes notice of her heart and beauty and offers to redeem Naomi because of her. The kinsman redeemer is not redeeming Ruth, he is redeeming Naomi, her deceased husband and sons! Ruth is a bi-product of the redemption. This becomes clear when Boaz speaks with the man who is first in line to be their kinsman redeemer. When he discloses that Ruth will come with the package, the other man declines and gives the right of redemption to Boaz. The beauty of this story is that through the kindness of a non-Jew who left her "Moabitish" ways behind and served the people of YHVH, He honors her by allowing her to bring forth the child, Oved (whose name means "worshiper"or "servant") who is the grandfather of King David and is in the line of the Messiah Yeshua!

Now let's compare the story of Ruth to today. The Jewish people have suffered a great loss. They are grieving and bitter. They are in need of a kinsman redeemer. As Gentile believers in Yeshua, we must learn from Ruth, and as Don says "put aside our Moabitish ways" and serve the Jewish people. If you read this story, you will notice that she is told by Naomi to return to her mother's house and find security in the home of a new husband. Ruth chooses to step into the unknown, without security, as a stranger in a foreign land. Later, Naomi instructs her to lay at the feet of Boaz. When she is discovered there, Ruth asks Boaz to *"spread your robe over your handmaid."* The Hebrew word for robe here is "wings," signifying Boaz' talit (prayer shawl). The amazing significance of this can only be realized as we learn to embrace and come "under" the blessings of the Jewish people. Is this not our duty also, to "lay" or sit at the feet of Yeshua, come under His wings, and intercede for His people to be redeemed? Through our intercession, servant heart, and sincerity of blessing them without agendas or ulterior motives, we will usher in their true Kinsman Redeemer, Yeshua the Messiah. His people will be restored to joy and share in the birthing or bringing forth of YHVH's purposes for the world for both Jew and Gentile, one in Messiah!

Let's finish up our history lesson. We will find out how, unlike Ruth, our "Christian" history is not one of blessing the Jewish people, or of fully understanding YHVH's Plan of Redemption. After the Council of Nicea in 325 CE, the foundation of the "Christian Church" had been laid. The seeds of hatred toward the Jews would reap a harvest of pogroms, attempted annihilation, persecution, inquisition, and forced conversion. The Catholic Church would adopt a great number of pagan practices. Sabbath was changed to Sunday and the Feasts of YHVH adapted into pagan holidays. Even when Martin Luther ushered in the Reformation, he continued all of the traditions and especially hatred toward the Jewish people. It is amazing to read the following quote in consideration of a man who claimed to preach "grace" and was the forerunner of Protestantism. In 1543 Luther published *On the Jews and Their Lies* in which he says that the Jews are a *"base, whoring people, that is, no people of God, and their boast of lineage, circumcision, and law must be accounted as filth."* They are full of the *"devil's feces ... which they wallow in like swine."* The synagogue was a *"defiled bride, yes, an incorrigible whore and an evil slut ..."* He argues that their synagogues and schools be set on fire, their prayer books destroyed, rabbis forbidden to preach, homes razed, and property and money confiscated. They should be shown no mercy or kindness, afforded no legal protection, and these *"poisonous envenomed worms"* should be drafted into forced labor or expelled for all time. He also seems to advocate their murder, writing *"we are at fault in not slaying them."*[2] Hitler used Martin Luther's writings against the Jews as part of his reasoning to annihilate them!

The only reason I have quoted this particular diatribe is because my heritage is Lutheran! I can only repent in sack cloth and ashes for the sins of my forefathers. Anti-semitism runs deep in the hearts of those who do not understand YHVH's Plan of Redemption. If you come from a mainstream church background, it is very likely that you have a deeply rooted anti-semitic spirit that you may not be aware of. It has caused a "veil" to come over your spiritual eyes so that you have been unable to discern the false and un-biblical traditions in your church calendar. It has also given you a sense of superiority over the Jewish people. If you cannot cry over what the Christian Religion did to the Jews, then you are missing a foundation stone of your faith. This is one reason I no longer call myself a "Christian." I do not believe the term "Christian" was meant to be the title given to followers or believers in Yeshua. Now the term is so loosely used and has such a broad definition, it no longer represents true followers of the Messiah. I prefer to be called a "Disciple of Yeshua," one who is learning and desiring to be like Him.

I will share a prayer that should be prayed out loud to break the covenant we have unconsciously made with the adversary. His whole purpose is to "kill, steal, and destroy." He has done a good job and he has had the help of those who have done it in the "name of Jesus Christ." Father forgive us!

Prayer of Repentance and Renunciation
by Joy Schneider

Father, God, the God of Abraham, Isaac, and Jacob, I repent and ask for Your forgiveness for my sins and the sins of my forefathers against Your people, the Jews. I acknowledge I have been ignorant and negligent concerning my sin and the sin of my forefathers. I repent for any beliefs and actions that have come through teachings of those who have spoken and testified against Your chosen people. I repent for words, thoughts and actions of hate, bitterness, revenge, torture and murder. I ask for Your forgiveness and mercy, O God. I ask for the Blood of Yeshua HaMashiach to wash my hands and heart from any and all anti-Semitism against the Jewish people and the nation of Israel, and to cleanse me from sin. I ask for the precious Blood of Yeshua to cleanse me from generational curses that have come upon my life and my household because of those who hated the ancestral line of Abraham. I call on the covenant of the cross of Calvary that cleanses me from sin and redeems me from the curse of the law. I ask for my heart to be transformed into Your heart for Israel and the Jewish people. I shut every door of entry that has been open to the enemy. I renounce and expose every anti-Semitic religious spirit that has disguised and hidden itself in the belief systems, doctrine and practices in my life, my church. I proclaim the Light of the glorious Gospel of

Yeshua HaMashiach against every false doctrine and lie. I renounce any "hook" of control or bondage satan has had in my life, and in the lives of my household, because of anti-Semitism in my life or in my background. I praise You that Your promise remains. I bless Israel and the Jewish people. I speak love, acceptance, and provision to Your people, the Jews. Lord, according to Your promise to Abraham, because I bless the Jews, I will be blessed. I call forth the covenant promises in my life and into the lives of my household and to my future generations. I confess that I am of the Seed of Abraham through Yeshua HaMashiach. I declare that I am redeemed from the curse. Thank You for Your mercy and grace. In Yeshua's Name, Amen.[3]

I invite you to do more archeology of your own roots. Where does it lead you? We must go one step further into more muddy and putrid decay before we can rise up out of the mire and be set upon the Rock of Yeshua!

----

[1] Don Finto, *Your People Shall Be My People*, Regal Books/Gospel Light, 2001, www.regalbooks.com, pg 19, emphasis mine. I highly recommend this book as well as others listed in the "Recommended Reading" section in the back of this book.

[2] Martin Luther, "On the Jews and Their Lies," *Luthers Werke*, 47:268-271; Translated by Martin H. Bertram in *Luther's Works*, Philadelphia: Fortress Press, 1971. Also cited in Robert Michael's "Luther, Luther Scholars, and the Jews," *Encounter 46* (Autumn 1985) No. 4:343-344, and in Hitler's book, *Mein Kampf.*

[3] Joy A. Schneider, *Identifying the Hierarchy of Satan*, Water of Life Unlimited, Fort Collins, Colorado, 2002. It is embedded in Chapter 14 "Abraham's Covenant." It is used with her permission. I exchanged her use of "Jesus Christ" with Yeshua HaMashiach.

11

Something Got Lost in Tradition

My people perish for a lack of knowledge. (Hosea 4:6)

Woe to those who call evil good and good evil, who
change darkness into light and light into darkness,
who change bitter into sweet and sweet into bitter!
Woe to those seeing themselves as wise, esteeming
themselves as clever. ... Therefore, as fire licks up the
stubble, and the chaff is consumed in the flame; so
their root will rot, and their flowers scatter like dust;
because they have rejected the Torah of ADONAI-
Tzva'ot, they have despised the word of the Holy
One of Isra'el. (Isaiah 5:20-21,24)

And their reverence for Me consists of tradition
learned by rote. (Isaiah 29:13b NASB)

The P'rushim and some of the Torah-teachers who
had come from Yerushalayim gathered together
with Yeshua and saw that some of his talmidim ate
with ritually unclean hands, that is, without doing
n'tilat-yadayim. (For the P'rushim, and indeed all
the Judeans, holding fast to the Tradition of the
Elders, do not eat unless they have given their hands
a ceremonial washing. Also, when they come from
the marketplace they do not eat unless they have
rinsed their hands up to the wrist; and they adhere
to many other traditions, such as washing cups, pots

and bronze vessels.) The P'rushim and the Torah-teachers asked him, "Why don't your talmidim live in accordance with the Tradition of the Elders, but instead eat with ritually unclean hands?" Yeshua answered them, "Yesha`yahu was right when he prophesied about you hypocrites—as it is written, 'These people honor me with their lips, but their hearts are far away from me. Their worship of me is useless, because they teach man-made rules as if they were doctrines.' You depart from God's command and hold onto human tradition. Indeed," he said to them, "you have made a fine art of departing from God's command in order to keep your tradition! For Moshe said, 'Honor your father and your mother,' and 'Anyone who curses his father or mother must be put to death.' But you say, 'If someone says to his father or mother, "I have promised as a korban [that is, as a gift to God] what I might have used to help you," ' then you no longer let him do anything for his father or mother. Thus, with your tradition which you had handed down to you, you nullify the Word of God! And you do other things like this."

(Mark 7: 1-13)

Have nothing to do with [NASB: Do not participate in] the deeds produced by darkness, but instead expose them, for it is shameful even to speak of the things these people do in secret. But everything exposed to the light is revealed clearly for what it is, since anything revealed is a light.

(Ephesians 5:11-14a)

Watch out, so that no one will take you captive by means of philosophy and empty deceit, following human tradition which accords with the elemental

SOMETHING GOT LOST IN TRADITION

spirits of the world but does not accord with the Messiah. (Colossians 2:8)

Several years ago I was struggling with an issue that I needed to "get the mind of the Lord" on. We were in Maine. It was winter. So, I donned my snowshoes and took a long walk in the woods. If you have never been in the north country where snow is on the ground from November to April, you may not realize how beautiful winter can be. As long as you wear warm enough gear, you can be outside. In the area of Maine we are from, winters are crisp and cold and the sky is as blue as the ocean in Hawaii. It is a wonderful place to clear your head and do some heart work.

The issue I was struggling with was Easter. I had learned the Feasts of the Lord. Somehow I would try to "combine" the two traditions of Passover and Easter (which I called "Resurrection Day") together. That particular year I could not combine them because they were in two different months! I liked to fellowship with Christians from time to time because in Maine there are very few "Sabbath keepers" and we were in a remote area where there was only one fairly "alive" church. I wanted to go to the Easter sunrise service the next morning, the breakfast afterward, and the service following. But I was torn. I realized I was compromising my true belief about the holiday, but I couldn't figure out what to do. Fellowship is good. Why not just participate with them. They are praising the Lord and acknowledging "Jesus." What is the matter with that?

Only the Spirit of YHVH had the answer and I knew I had to get it straight from Him. There are times when we must just "get with God." This was one of those times. As I crunched through the deep snow in the woods, Scriptures began to pour into my mind. I heard the Father say to me, "No, you cannot participate in Easter ever again. I want you to go back and study the origins of all the traditions and holidays of the Christian church." I had my answer. I said, "Yes, sir."

Shortly thereafter I called my Mother to ask her about the traditions surrounding this holiday. Her answer reminded me of the above Scriptures when she replied, "It's tradition." She was acknowledging that we do these things because we always have done them and have never asked why.

Some of you may not be aware that there is a possible issue with Christmas, Easter, and all the other holidays that are on the Christian calendar. A closer look will reveal some origins from paganism that were blatantly incorporated in the new religion of Christianity in order to deliberately veer from any flavor of Jewishness. The difficult thing to come to grips with, is that much of what was being expelled was not exclusively Jewish. It was Biblical. Theology has "explained away" all of these issues by the "cover all" statement, "We are no longer under the law." We have covered some of this in the previous chapters, but now we need to address some of the details.

This chapter is going to be hard for those deeply steeped in a Christian tradition. The root goes very deep and things have been in place and engrained for so long that to touch the root is going to be very painful. Be prepared with some healing balm because this will challenge the way "church" has been done for centuries![1]

So, what am I saying? That food sacrificed to idols has any significance in itself? or that an idol has significance in itself? No, what I am saying is that the things which pagans sacrifice, they sacrifice not to God but to demons; and I don't want you to become sharers of the demons! You can't drink both a cup of the Lord and a cup of demons, you can't partake in both a meal of the Lord and a meal of demons. Or are we trying to make the Lord jealous? We aren't stronger than he is, are we? "Everything is permitted," you say? Maybe, but not everything is

helpful. "Everything is permitted?" Maybe, but not everything is edifying. (I Corinthians 10:19-23)

My personal belief is that when we participate in certain holidays and practices that have a decisive pagan origin, we may be "opening a door" for the adversary in our homes and in our families. This would give a legal right for the enemy to torment us. Perhaps we need to examine ourselves and ask the Father to reveal any origins of darkness to us. I always pray that I could be like Yeshua when He said that the enemy had nothing in Him (John 14:30).

This is where knowledge of Torah is so powerful. For example, when you read:

Don't bring something abhorrent into your house, or you will share in the curse that is on it; instead, you are to detest it completely, loathe it utterly; for it is set apart for destruction. (Deuteronomy 7:26)

I do not believe that is a legalistic observance of Torah. I believe that is a loving heavenly Father wanting to protect His kids because He knows how devious the enemy stalking "like a roaring lion looking for someone to devour" is! (I Peter 5:8)

I became angry as I began to uncover the truth of the "Christian" traditions and holidays. I felt deceived and lied to. I must admit, the Lord has had to temper my temper these past years to give me His perspective on all of this. I wanted to be like Yeshua with the whip and the money changers. *"Clear the Temple!!"* My biggest question to Him was, "Why did you let it happen?"

Do you remember the earlier phrase "then man began...." If you read the book of Hosea, you will see a picture of Israel as the harlot. YHVH is using Hosea to give a picture of His bride going her own way. She's gone off to other lovers. He is going to abandon her for a time.

111

I will end her happiness, her festivals, Rosh-Hodesh [New Moons], and shabbats, and all her designated times. (Hosea 2:11)

When I read the above verse I felt I had my answer. Part of the judgment of Israel was the depriving of their Feasts and Shabbats. Did YHVH really allow syncretism of the holidays because of Israel or was this a picture of the "church" as YHVH would see it develop. I believe it is both.

Rather, what I did order them was this: "Pay attention to what I say. Then I will be your God, and you will be my people. In everything, live according to the way that I order you, so that things will go well for you." But they neither listened nor paid attention, but lived according to their own plans, in the stubbornness of their evil hearts, thus going backward and not forward. (Jeremiah 7:23-24)

You see much but don't pay attention; you open your ears, but you don't listen. (Isaiah 42:20)

In the ninth year of Hoshea, the king of Ashur captured Shomron. He carried Isra'el away captive to Ashur, resettling them in Halach, in Havor on the Gozan River and in the cities of the Medes. This came about because the people of Isra'el had sinned against ADONAI their God, who had brought them out of the land of Egypt, out from under the domination of Pharaoh king of Egypt. They feared other gods and lived by the customs of the nations that ADONAI had expelled ahead of the people of Isra'el and by those of the kings of Isra'el. The people of Isra'el secretly did things that were not right, according to ADONAI their God. They built high places for themselves wherever they lived, from the watchtower to the fortified city. They set up standing-stones and sacred poles for themselves on any high hill and under any green tree. Then they would make offerings on all the high places, like the nations ADONAI had expelled ahead of them, and would do wicked things to provoke the anger of ADONAI; moreover, they served idols, something ADONAI had expressly told them not to do. ADONAI had warned Isra'el and Y'hudah in advance through every prophet and seer, "Turn from your evil ways; and obey my mitzvot and regulations, in accordance with the entire Torah which I ordered your ancestors to keep and which I sent to you through my servants the prophets." Nevertheless, they refused to listen but made themselves as stubborn as their ancestors, who did not put their trust in ADONAI their God. Thus they rejected his laws; his covenant, which he had made with their ancestors; and the solemn warnings he had given them. Instead they pursued worthless things and became worthless themselves, imitating the nations around them, whom ADONAI had ordered them not to emulate..... They both feared ADONAI and served their own gods in the manner customary among the nations from which they had been taken away. To this day they continue to follow their former [pagan] customs. They do not fear ADONAI. They do not follow the regulations, rulings, Torah or mitzvah which ADONAI ordered the descendants of Ya'akov, to whom he gave the name Isra'el, with whom ADONAI had made a covenant and charged them, "Do not fear other gods or bow down to them, serve them or sacrifice to them. On the contrary, you are to fear ADONAI, who brought you out of the land of Egypt with great

power and an outstretched arm. **Worship him, and
sacrifice to him. You are to** <u>observe forever</u> **the laws,
rulings, Torah and mitzvah which he wrote for you.
You are not to fear other gods, and you are not to
forget the covenant I made with you. No, you must
not fear other gods but must fear ADONAI your God;
then he will rescue you from the power of all your
enemies."** <u>However, they didn't listen, but followed
their old [pagan] practices</u>. **(II Kings 17:6-15, 33-40)**

The issue at stake for Israel was what is known in
Hebrew as "Avota zara"—Avota from the root word "work"
and Zara from "stranger." It is translated as "foreign worship." [2]
Israel was not to even learn about the religions of the nations
surrounding them. They were to be "set apart"—Holy unto the
Lord. They never were able to achieve that as a nation. There
was always a "remnant" of individuals who obeyed YHVH,
but for the most part, the people were followers, like sheep,
and went astray.

**We all, like sheep, went astray; we turned, each one,
to his own way; yet ADONAI laid on him the guilt of
all of us. (Isaiah 53:6)**

If we look honestly at the Christian church of today, what
is the difference between us and Israel? I see no difference.
We already spoke of keeping our "Moabitish" or Gentile ways.
We are the nations Israel was not to learn the ways of! We, like
Israel, have been brought out of bondage and slavery. We were
given a set of instructions by YHVH Himself through His Son,
Yeshua. He came to represent the very heart of the Father and
bestow upon us His Spirit to teach us. Did we listen to His
voice or to others?

I could spend pages upon pages detailing "pagan" practices in the church.[3] I could accuse the Catholic church and Christianity's founding fathers for incorporating pagan practices to make Christianity more favorable to the people, but I am not going to do that. I will make recommendations for books and places you can research yourself. I will include a chart at the end of the book for those interested, but I cannot blame anyone but myself if I didn't look into it or go to the Father and ask what *He* wanted. If I chose not to "hear his voice" and listen and obey, then the buck stops here.

Everything I need to know is found in the Word of YHVH and in a personal relationship with Him, confirmed by His Word. If I study the original I should know when a counterfeit appears. If I want to know the origin of the name Easter and why it is important to not use that name, than I should ask the question. I should not be accepting tradition, even if those traditions are centuries old and have been Christianized. If I were a pastor of a Christian church, I would hope I would have the courage to declare to my congregation: *"We will no longer use the name Easter for our Resurrection celebration because that is the name of a goddess and we do not serve the queen of heaven, we serve the King of Kings and Lord of Lords whose resurrection we celebrate."*

... then be careful not to forget ADONAI, who brought you out of the land of Egypt, where you lived as slaves. You are to fear ADONAI your God, serve him and swear by his name. You are not to follow other gods, chosen from the gods of the peoples around you; because ADONAI, your God, who is here with you, is a jealous God.... (Deuteronomy 6:12-15a)

Yes, they defiled my holy name by the disgusting practices they committed; which is why I destroyed them in my anger. (Ezekiel 43:8b)

Yeshua's challenge to the religious leaders of His day was against their traditions, not Torah. I hope you can hear what YHVH is saying to the "church" of today who claim to be the "Bride of Christ." You have to believe me when I say that I am crying when I write this. The grief of the Father is so deep that it can hardly be expressed. He lets me feel it sometimes as nausea, sometimes as travailing cries. By breaking from the Jewish believers who "birthed" the church, a spirit of division has created over 20,000 separate denominations![4] This is the kind of fruit the "Christian church" has been bearing, not the *"peaceful fruit of righteousness"* (Hebrews 12:11 NASB) and as my husband Ronald would query, *"How's that working for you?"*

To the Western Constantinian Christian church who has become like Israel—the harlot. You are the church of Laodicea. Laodicea means "voice of the people." Here is what the Spirit says:

To the angel of the Messianic Community [most versions use "church"] in Laodicea, write: Here is the message from the Amen, the faithful and true witness, the Ruler of God's creation: "I know what you are doing: you are neither cold nor hot. How I wish you were either one or the other! So, because you are lukewarm, neither cold nor hot, I will vomit you out of my mouth! For you keep saying, 'I am rich, I have gotten rich, I don't need a thing!' You don't know that you are the one who is wretched, pitiable, poor, blind and naked! My advice to you is to buy from me gold refined by fire, so that you may be rich; and white clothing, so that you may be dressed and not have to be ashamed of your nakedness; and eyesalve to rub on your eyes, so that you may see. As for me, I rebuke and discipline everyone I love; so exert yourselves, and turn from your sins! Here, I'm

standing at the door, knocking. If someone hears my
voice and opens the door, I will come in to him and
eat with him, and he will eat with me. I will let him
who wins the victory sit with me on my throne, just
as I myself also won the victory and sat down with
my Father on his throne. Those who have ears, let
them hear what the Spirit is saying to the Messianic
communities." (Revelation 3:14-22)

If you are willing, we are now ready to expose the bottom
layer. We're ready to reveal the answer as to why the Name of
Yeshua is important.

----

[1] I need to say that I have met some truly beautiful, Godly, deeply spiritual,
dedicated followers of Jesus who have never known of these things. I do
not condemn anyone for past practice, however, when truth is exposed, one
must consider future participation. Please consider these things prayerfully.
Put on your snowshoes or your sandals and "get with God" to find out what
He requires of you.

[2] There are many sources that expose the Pagan origins of Christian
traditions. Two of the many books I have read that were very enlightening
were: *The Two Babylons* by Rev. Alexander Hislop, Presbyterian Free
Church of Scotland, 1919, —an old English volume—quite tedious but well
worth the effort. It can be found on line at: http://www.biblebelievers.com/
babylon/00index.htm; and *Pagan Christianity?* by Frank Viola and George
Barnam, Tyndale House Publishers, Inc., Carol Stream, IL, 2002,2008,
http://www.paganchristianity.org/ I do not personally endorse all that these
books share, but I believe it is an eye opener for those who wish to bury
their head in the sand and pretend paganism doesn't exist in the "church."
   For a good study on this topic, First Fruits of Zion has a CD set called
"What about Paganism" by Toby Janicki. Although I do not come out at
the same place they do concerning the holidays, the study gives a good
background on the subject: www.ffoz.org

[3] A table of holidays commonly observed by the Church, their origins in
the occult and how they are applied to the Christian church can be found in
Appendix B.

[4] Various sources indicate the number can be anywhere from 20,000-40,000 since 30 CE. The point is that it is far too many to count!

12

Exposed!

In the year of King 'Uziyahu's death I saw Adonai sitting on a high, lofty throne! The hem of his robe filled the temple. S'rafim stood over him, each with six wings - two for covering his face, two for covering his feet and two for flying. They were crying out to each other, "More holy than the holiest holiness is ADONAI-Tzva'ot! The whole earth is filled with his glory!" The doorposts shook at the sound of their shouting, and the house was filled with smoke. Then I said, "Woe to me! I [too] am doomed! {undone, exposed, lost, ruined} because I, a man with unclean lips, living among a people with unclean lips, have seen with my own eyes the King, ADONAI-Tzva'ot!" One of the s'rafim flew to me with a glowing coal in his hand, which he had taken with tongs from the altar. He touched my mouth with it and said, "Here! This has touched your lips. Your iniquity is gone, your sin is atoned for." Then I heard the voice of Adonai saying, "Whom should I send? Who will go for us?" I answered, "I'm here, send me!" He said, "Go and tell this people: 'Yes, you hear, but you don't understand. You certainly see, but you don't get the point!' "Make the heart of this people [sluggish with] fat, stop up their ears, and shut their eyes. Otherwise, seeing with their eyes, and hearing with their ears, then understanding with their hearts, they might repent and be healed!" (Isaiah 6:1-10 − my emphasis and paraphrase in {})

For the leader. By David: Fools say in their hearts, "There is no God."They deal corruptly, their deeds are vile, not one does what is right. From heaven ADONAI observes humankind to see if anyone has understanding, if anyone seeks God. But all turn aside, all alike are corrupt; no one does what is right, not a single one. Don't they ever learn, all those evildoers, who eat up my people as if eating bread and never call on ADONAI? There they are, utterly terrified; for God is with those who are righteous. You may mock the plans of the poor, but their refuge is ADONAI. How I wish Isra'el's salvation would come out of Tziyon! When ADONAI restores his people's fortunes, Ya'akov will rejoice, Isra'el will be glad! (Psalm 14)

My husband, Ronald, has an older cousin (now deceased) whom most would have considered a "saint." He was totally sold out to the Lord, walked in gifts of prophesy and words of knowledge. He was a humble, wise man of God and served Him faithfully. He did nothing unless he "heard from the Father." He related to Ronald one time that he was sitting in his chair at home and conversing with the Lord about things. The Lord said to him "You have never done anything good." He said, "Really? What about this and what about that?" He continued to list all of the "good" things he felt he had done in service to the Lord. As he became silent, the Lord gently spoke to him a profound and deep truth. "You have done things. I made them good." It "rocked his world" as the teens would say these days. He felt like Isaiah—"I am undone, I am exposed." Wasn't God right? That is why He says in both Psalm 14 and Psalm 53:

"From heaven ADONAI observes humankind to see if anyone has understanding, if anyone seeks God.

But all turn aside, all alike are corrupt; no one does
what is right, not a single one." (Psalm 14:2)

God looks out from heaven upon the human race
to see if even one is wise, if even one seeks God.
Every one of them is unclean, altogether corrupt;
not one of them does what is good, not a single one.
(Psalm 53:2-3)

You may say "but not me!"

The heart is more deceitful than anything else and
mortally sick. Who can fathom it? I, ADONAI,
search the heart; I test inner motivations; in order
to give to everyone what his actions and conduct
deserve. (Jeremiah 17:9-10)

Up until now we have been digging into history and
facts. We have been sifting through the rubble of our past.
Some of it has hurt to read and some of it we just don't care
about and discard in the rubble pile. We have been asking the
question, "What does it matter? God knows my heart. What
does it matter what name I call Him or His Son?" I have asked
myself that question for years. I kept grappling with it and
searching and seeking and digging. I know wonderful Godly
men and women who have lived their lives totally surrendered
to Him. You may be one of them. This is why this will be
hard to share. Most people who pick up a book like this have
open, teachable hearts and my desire is not to "trample" on
anyone's heart here! I feel a deep sense that YHVH is exposing
something that I hadn't even thought about until I was writing
this book. I told Him that I could not continue until I had the
answer. I was not expecting what He told me.

Here is what I sense the Father revealing to me. It is
not about what we name God or His Son, because YHVH is

merciful and gracious, and infinitely patient with us. He is *more, other,* and outside of our human "stuff." He looks at hearts and knows when someone is "calling on His Name," no matter what name they use, BUT, **it is what it exposes in us.**

I am asking that you take the time to ask yourself if the following observations are true or false. Only the Spirit of YHVH can reveal truth, so I am suggesting that before you begin this portion, please ask Him to reveal the truth of your own heart to you. There does not need to be any condemnation, but conviction is a work of the Spirit and will always lead to repentance, if we allow it.

For Christians, it may expose the deeply rooted pride and arrogance of Replacement Theology, the Anti-semitism of your religion, or the fact that you have accepted 1700+ years of "tradition" and have not really gotten to *know* your Savior. You claim to be the "bride of Christ" but you didn't find out that your bridegroom is Jewish and has a Hebrew name and that "Christ" is not His last name, but is His Title meaning *Anointed One* or *Messiah.*

You didn't ask yourself the deep questions about your religious traditions that contradict the Bible. You have looked at the Scriptures through the lens of your current world view, or "from the cross on" instead of asking the Spirit of YHVH to reveal His purposes and truth to you from Genesis 1 forward. You read the New Covenant Scriptures through the lens of your modern Western Greek Christian culture instead of getting in touch with the foundation and the Biblical roots of your faith.

Would we be able to consider the two trees in the garden?[1] The one being the Tree of the Knowledge of Good and Evil; the other the Tree of Life. What is the source of our knowledge? Is it from YHVH and His Word of Life? Or is it knowledge from man? Who are we seeking truth from? Are we willing to die to our version of the truth and confess that we have eaten far too long from the Tree of The Knowledge of Good And Evil and have forsaken the Tree of Life? We have become perfecters of our own "truth" to such an extent that we have missed the life of the Spirit of Truth! Can we admit we changed a Jewish Messiah into a Greek Gentile Savior and in changing His name through Greek transliteration, a great divide in thought and culture began? Every cult and diversion from the true faith has developed because it wasn't rooted and grounded in the proper tree.

If you are Jewish and you don't know Yeshua, then it may expose deeply rooted bitterness, resentment, and unforgiveness of a past history of what others have done to you and your people, or deeper still, the hatred from a religion that completely refuses to acknowledge the possibility of Yeshua as the Messiah and persecutes those who have accepted Him as the Messiah of Israel. You have refused to seek YHVH Himself and ask His opinion. You will gladly accept a Jewish person who doesn't even believe in God (an atheist) and say he can still be Jewish, but you won't let a Messianic believer in Yeshua who is "shomer Torah" (Torah observant) to continue to be Jewish! You claim he has "changed religions." What kind of fruit is the tree bearing? Can you lay aside all the years, and all the persecution, and look with fresh eyes and a new perspective? Are you willing to consider YHVH's judgment in light of His Covenant and the subsequent blessings and curses for Israel? Are you willing to ask the Spirit of YHVH to reveal the truth to you and like the above challenge to your Gentile neighbors eat from the Tree of Life?

Many people hesitate to go a different direction, or go against family (tradition) because they fear what other people will think or do.

As they were traveling on the road, a man said to him, "I will follow you wherever you go." Yeshua answered him, "The foxes have holes, and the birds flying about have nests, but the Son of Man has no home of his own." To another he said, "Follow me!" but the man replied, "Sir, first let me go away and bury my father." Yeshua said, "Let the dead bury their own dead; you, go and proclaim the Kingdom of God!" Yet another said, "I will follow you, sir, but first let me say good-by to the people at home." To him Yeshua said, "No one who puts his hand to the plow and keeps looking back is fit to serve in the Kingdom of God." (Luke 9:57-62)

Yeshua also said:

So do not fear them; for there is nothing covered that will not be uncovered, or hidden that will not be known. What I tell you in the dark, speak in the light; what is whispered in your ear, proclaim on the housetops. "Do not fear those who kill the body but are powerless to kill the soul. Rather, fear him who can destroy both soul and body in Gei-Hinnom.... Whoever loves his father or mother more than he loves me is not worthy of me; anyone who loves his son or daughter more than he loves me is not worthy of me. And anyone who does not take up his execution-stake and follow me is not worthy of me. Whoever finds his own life will lose it, but the person who loses his life for my sake will find it. "Whoever receives you is receiving me, and whoever receives me is receiving the One who sent me.
(Matthew 10: 26-28, 37-40)

I find that the deeper I dig and the more I ask the Spirit to reveal truth to me, the more I uncover my own motivations.

This is why Yeshua challenged the religious leaders of the day. Were they doing things out of love for YHVH or out of tradition? Were they doing it for show or attention, or out of sincerity? Were they giving from a heart of thanksgiving, or were they giving to receive? What Yeshua was doing was exposing their motives. What the Spirit of YHVH is doing is exposing us.

The beautiful thing about this is that He is not "up there" waiting to pound us down with a stick and say "bad boy" or "bad girl." He provides a way for us to come to Him and be forgiven. Then He says to us, like Yeshua said to the woman caught in adultery *"Go and sin no more"* (John 8:11). It becomes our choice if we will obey or stray. He loves us that much.

There are many hurting people in this world. You may be one of them. You may have been hurt by the church, or people who call themselves "Christians." You may have been wounded by people who were supposed to be your safety, such as parents or spouses. You may be disillusioned because you see hypocrisy in every religious institution and person who calls themselves "Christian." You may be a Palestinian Christian, caught in a position of strife with two people groups surrounding you. On the one hand you have the Muslims who are oppressing you and on the other hand you have the Israelis who are also in a position of power over you and it often feels like oppression as well. In addition, you have the mainstream "church" telling you that Israel has been replaced and they have no right to be in the land, that they are no longer YHVH's chosen people.

Regardless of the political or religious situation around you, if you call yourself a "Christian" you must go back to your Scriptures and study what Yeshua says about loving your enemies and praying for those who persecute you (Matthew 5-7). To bless Israel does not mean you agree with everything the political state of Israel is doing. To bless Israel means to bless her people and to do good to them, regardless; to extend mercy because you have received mercy.

Just as you yourselves were disobedient to God before but have received mercy, now because of Israel's disobedience; so also Israel has been disobedient now, so that by your showing them the same mercy that God has shown you, they too may now receive God's mercy. (Romans 11:30-31)

We are to be the example of Yeshua to the world of Muslims, Christians, Jews, and all other peoples. In every case, there is an answer. It is Yeshua. It is getting to know Him and asking for His help. He is your salvation. He is the only one!

Even those who do know the Name Yeshua and use it, who have uncovered the Biblical Feasts and Sabbath—ie: Messianic believers, it would be good to ask yourself the question—Do I really know Yeshua? Or do I just know about Him? We can all be followers of anything. Is it authentic? Are there "signs following" in your life? (Mark 16:14-20)

Even in Messianic Judaism, it appears like some are trying to build another "building" that looks and acts a lot like the Gentile Greek Christian church. On the other hand, others of you are trying to be so "Jewish" that Gentiles are excluded or meant to feel inferior. The goal of our faith should not be to make everyone "Messianic" or "Christian"—it is to return to the original purpose of creation—relationship with the creator YHVH—to become like Yeshua. The Apostle Sha'ul said it best in Philippians 3:

For it is we who are the Circumcised, we who worship by the Spirit of God and make our boast in the Messiah Yeshua! <u>We do not put confidence in human qualifications</u>.... But the things that used to be advantages for me, I have, because of the Messiah, come to consider a disadvantage. Not only that, but <u>I consider everything a disadvantage in comparison with the supreme value of knowing the Messiah Yeshua as my Lord. It was because of him that I gave up everything and regard it all as garbage, in order to gain the Messiah and be found in union with him, not having any righteousness of my own based on legalism, but having that righteousness which comes through the Messiah's faithfulness, the righteousness from God based on trust.</u> Yes, I gave it all up in order to know him, that is, to know the power of his resurrection and the fellowship of his sufferings as I am being conformed to his death, so that somehow I might arrive at being resurrected from the dead. It is not that I have already obtained it or already reached the goal—no, I keep pursuing it in the hope of taking hold of that for which the Messiah Yeshua took hold of me. Brothers, I, for my part, do not think of myself as having yet gotten hold of it; but one thing I do: forgetting what is behind me and straining forward toward what lies ahead, I keep pursuing the goal in order to win the prize offered by God's upward calling in the Messiah Yeshua. Therefore, as many of us as are mature, let us keep paying attention to this; and if you are differently minded about anything, God will also reveal this to you. (Philippians 3:3,7-15)

One new man is not Jew or Gentile. It is righteousness in Yeshua.

For Gentiles who have "come out of the church," Moshe at the Shorashim shop in the Old City of Jerusalem has said, "Don't spit in the well that fed you all these years." There are men and women of YHVH in the "Christian" church who love Him with all their hearts. We are called to honor the true brethren no matter what denomination they adhere to. We must be very careful in our judgments. As much as we would like to awaken the rest of the "Constantinian Christian Church" and see a transformation, we may get frustrated when they do not see what we see or respond as we have responded. They may become even more set in their ways. Just remember where you came from. Extend mercy. Educate by example. Love. Serve. Be a blessing. Pray for the veils to be removed from the nations. Don't compromise the Sabbath or Yeshua's Name. Celebrate the Feasts and invite others to join you. Spread the Good News of the Gospel of Yeshua. You are the fulfillment of Isaiah 58:12 *"You will rebuild the ancient ruins, raise foundations from ages past, and be called 'Repairer of broken walls, Restorer of streets to live in.'"*

It's time to uncover His Name in the Scriptures. Let's sell all we have, find the pearl of great price, and then move on to victory!

----

[1] "There were Two Trees in the Garden," Art Katz, audio message found at http://artkatzministries.org/audio-messages/there-were-two-trees-in-the-garden-2-part-series/ I have never heard messages that have "cut me to the quick" as these by Art Katz. Although he is no longer with us, his ministry continues through the availability of the internet. There are so many others to recommend, but this one is a great study.

13

Yeshua in the TaNaKH

The Kingdom of Heaven is like a treasure hidden in a field. A man found it, hid it again, then in great joy went and sold everything he owned, and bought that field. Again, the Kingdom of Heaven is like a merchant on the lookout for fine pearls. On finding one very valuable pearl he went away, sold everything he owned and bought it. (Matthew 13:44-46)

Yeshua said to them, "This is what I meant when I was still with you and told you that everything written about me in the Torah of Moshe, the Prophets and the Psalms had to be fulfilled." Then he opened their minds, so that they could understand the Tanakh, telling them, "Here is what it says: the Messiah is to suffer and to rise from the dead on the third day; and in his name repentance leading to forgiveness of sins is to be proclaimed to people from all nations, starting with Yerushalayim." (Luke 24:44-45)

We have explored the Hebrew origins of Yeshua's name, explored the meaning of transliteration, translation, and dug through some pretty mucky history. We saw our own reflection in the bottom of the pit and we have repented of our arrogance, our pride, our unforgiveness, or our anti-Semitism. We are ready to see the real Yeshua in the Scriptures and to celebrate His salvation in our own lives. We have put off our "religious" mantle. We have exchanged our filthy rags of self righteousness and allowed the Holy Spirit to wash us clean and fresh in His Spirit and robe us in His righteousness. Now let's soak in the Scriptures.

When you read the Hebrew Scriptures, Yeshua's Name continues to pop out all over the pages. This is one reason why it is important to restore His name. These verses reveal His reputation! Even if you are just reading the Bible in English, you can see it when you see the word "salvation." The following is a list of Scriptures that have His name hidden in the verses. We have already defined the full meaning of ישועה yeshuah. Let us review. ישועה yeshuah is from ישע yasha, which is a primary root: *to be open, wide, or free, to be safe, to free, defend, deliver, help, preserve, rescue, bring salvation, get victory.* Yeshua as a name from Yahoshua means YHVH is our *salvation, deliverance, aid, victory, prosperity, health, and help.* I transliterated the word "salvation" into the form of yeshuah used in the Hebrew. The pronouns and conjunctions are part of the Hebrew word and therefore included as well. (ie: "for your salvation" is one word in the Hebrew, therefore the transliteration would be "l'yeshuatach" with the "ch" pronounced as a soft "k" or hard "h.") For the B'rit Hadasha (New Covenant) section, the appropriate word is simply bolded.

Unless otherwise marked, all verses in TaNaKH portion of this section are quoted from <u>A Literal Translation of the Bible</u> from <u>The Interlinear Bible</u>, 1-volume edition, second edition, copyright 1986 by Jay P. Green, Sr. (The author uses YHVH instead of Jehovah to honor the sacred personal name of God.) All verses in the B'rit Hadashah are taken from <u>The Complete Jewish Bible.</u>

Torah:

Genesis (B'resheet) 49:18 "I have waited for your <u>Salvation</u> (l'yeshuatach), O YHVH."

Exodus (Sh'mot)14:13 "And Moses said to the people 'Do not be afraid. Take your stand and see the <u>Salvation</u> (yeshuot) of YHVH which He will prepare for you today. For as you see the Egyptians today, you will not continue to see them again forever.' "

15:2 "My strength and song is YHVH and He has become <u>Salvation</u> (l'yeshuah) to me. This is my God (El), and I will glorify Him; the God (El) of my father and I will exalt Him."

Deuteronomy (D'varim) 32:15 "But Yeshurun grew fat and kicked. You grew fat, thick and stubborn. And he abandoned God (Elohay) who made him, and dishonored the rock of his <u>Salvation</u> (yeshuato)."

Nevi'im (Prophets):

I Samuel (Sh'mu'el Alef) 2:1-2 "And Hannah prayed and said: 'My heart has exalted in YHVH; my horn has been high in YHVH. My mouth has been large over my enemies; for I have rejoiced in Your <u>Salvation</u> (b'yeshuatecha). There is none Holy like YHVH, for there is none except you; Yea there is no rock like our God (El hayenu).' "

14:45 "…..shall Jonathan die, He who did this great <u>deliverance</u> (ha yeshuah) in Israel?"

II Samuel (Sh'mu'el Bet) 22:51 "A tower of <u>Salvation</u> (yeshuot) is He to His King; even doing mercy to His anointed, to David and to his seed, until forever! (od olam)."

Isaiah (Yeshayahu) 12:2 "Behold, God (El) is my <u>Salvation</u>! (yeshuati) I will trust and not be afraid, for my strength and song is Yah. YHVH; yea, He has become my salvation (l'yeshuah)."

12:3 "And you shall draw waters out of wells of <u>Salvation</u> (ha yeshuah) with joy."

25:9 "And one shall say in that day, Behold, this is our God; (Elohenu), we have waited for Him, and He will save us. This is YHVH; we have waited for Him; we will be glad and rejoice in His <u>Salvation</u> (b'yeshuato)."

26:1 "In that day this song shall be sung in the land of Judah: A strong city is ours; He sets up <u>Salvation</u> (yeshuah) as our walls and ramparts."

26:18 "We conceived; we writhe; as it were, we gave birth to wind. We have not worked <u>Salvation</u> (yeshuot) for the earth....."

33:2 "O YHVH, be gracious to us. We have hoped in You; be their arm in the mornings , our <u>Salvation</u> (yeshuatenu) also in time of distress."

33:6 "And He will be the security of your times, a wealth of <u>Salvation</u> (yeshuah), wisdom, and knowledge; the fear of YHVH is His treasure."

49:6 "... I will also give you for a light of the nations, that you might be My <u>Salvation</u> (yeshuati) to the end of the earth."

49:8 "So says YHVH: in a favorable time I have answered you, and in a day of <u>Salvation</u> (yeshuah) I have helped you...."

51:6 "... but my <u>Salvation </u>(yeshuati) shall be forever, and My righteousness shall not be broken."

52:7 "How beautiful on the mountains are the feet of him bringing good news, proclaiming Salvation (yeshuah); saying to Zion, Your God (El) reigns!"

52:10 "YHVH has bared His Holy arm in the eyes of all the nations; and all the ends of the earth shall see the Salvation (yeshuah) of our God (El)."

56:1 "So says YHVH; Keep justice and do righteousness, for My Salvation (yeshuati) is near to come, and My righteousness to be revealed."

59:11 "We all of us roar like bears, and we moan sadly like doves. We look for justice, but there is none; for Salvation (l'yeshuah), but it is far from us."

59:16-17 "And He saw that there was no man, and He was astonished that there was no intercessor. And His own arm saved for Him; and His righteousness sustained Him. For He put on righteousness like armor, and a helmet of Salvation (yeshuah) on His head. And He put on robes of vengeance as clothing; and He put on zeal like a mantle."

60:18 ".... but you shall call your walls, Salvation (yeshuah), and your gates, praise."

62:1 "For Zion's sake, I will not be silent; and for Jerusalem's sake, I will not rest; until her righteousness goes forth as brightness, and her Salvation (v'yeshuata) as a burning lamp."

62:11 "Behold, YHVH has made known to the end of the earth; Tell the daughter of Zion, Behold, your Salvation (yeshuach) comes! Behold, His reward is with Him, and His work before Him."

Jonah (Yonah) 2:9 "But I will sacrifice to You with the voice of thanksgiving; I will fulfill that which I have vowed. Salvation (yeshuata) belongs to YHVH!"

Habakkuk (Havakuk) 3:8,13 "... for You ride on horses; Your chariots of Salvation (yeshuah)." ... You went forth for the Salvation (l'yesha, a form of yeshuah) of Your people, for the Salvation (l'yesha) of Your anointed.

Writings:

Psalms (Tehillim) The Hebrew Tanakh uses a different numbering for the verses – hence (#)

Psalms 3:2 (3) "Many are the sayings of my soul, there is no Salvation (yeshuata) for him in God (Elohim). Selah"

3:8 (9) "Salvation (ha yeshuah) belongs to YHVH; (to YHVH is yeshuah) Your blessing is on your people. Selah"

9:14 (15) "So that I may declare all Your praises in the gates of the daughter of Zion; I will rejoice in Your Salvation (be yeshuatecha)"

13:5 "But I have trusted in Your mercy; my heart shall rejoice in Your Salvation (b'yeshuatecha)."

14:7 (8) "Who will bring the Salvation (yeshuat) of Israel out of Zion? When YHVH brings back the captivity of His people, Jacob shall rejoice; Israel shall be glad."

18:50 (51) "... magnifying the Salvations (yeshuaot) to His king, and working mercy to his anointed, to David and His seed forever."

20:5 (6) "We will rejoice in Your <u>Salvation</u> (be yeshuatecha), and we will set up banners in the Name of our God (Elohenu); may YHVH fulfill all your prayers."

21:1 (2) "The King rejoices in Your strength, O YHVH; and how greatly does he rejoice in Your <u>Salvation</u> (b'yeshuatecha)."

21:5 (6) "His Glory is great in Your <u>Salvation</u> (b'yeshuatecha); You have laid honor and majesty on him."

35:3 (4) "... say to my soul, I am your <u>Salvation</u> (yeshuatach ani)."

35:9 (10) "And my soul shall be joyful in ADONAI; it will rejoice in His <u>Salvation</u> (yeshuato)."

42:11 (12) "O my soul, why are you cast down? And why do you moan within me? Hope in God (Elohim), for I yet thank Him for the <u>Salvation</u> (yeshuah) of my face and my God (El)."

44:4 (5) "You are He, my King, O God (Elohim); command <u>deliverances</u> (yeshuot) for Jacob."

53:6 (7) "Who gives from Zion the <u>Salvation</u> (yeshuaot) of Israel?"

62:1 (2) "Only to God (Elohim) is my soul silent; from Him comes my <u>Salvation</u> (yeshuati)."

62:2 (3) "He alone is my rock and my <u>Salvation</u> (yeshuati), my strong tower; I shall not be greatly moved."

67:2 (3) "That Your way may be known on earth, Your <u>Salvation</u> (yeshuatecha) among all nations."

135

Psalms (cont.)

68:19-20 (20-21) "Blessed be the Lord: day by day He bears burdens for us, the God (ha El) of our Salvation (yeshuatenu). Selah. Our God (ha El) is the God (El) of Salvation (mosha'ah); and to YHVH the Lord are the issues of death."

69:29 (30) "But I am poor and in pain; O God (Elohim), Your Salvation (yeshuatecha) shall set me on high."

70:4 (5) "Let all those who seek You rejoice, and be glad in You; and let those who love Your Salvation (yeshuatecha) forever say, Let God (Elohim) be magnified."

74:12 (13) "For God (Elohim) is my King of old, who works Salvation (yeshuaot) in the midst of the land."

78:22 (23) "Because they did not believe in God (Elohim), and trusted not in His Salvation (b'yeshuato)."

88:1 (2) "O YHVH God (Elohei) of my Salvation (yeshuati), I have cried in the day, in the night before You."

89:26 (27) "He shall cry to Me, My Father (avi) You are my God (El), and the rock of my Salvation (yeshuati)."

91:16 "I will satisfy him, and will make him see, My Salvation (b'yeshuati)."

96:2 "Sing to YHVH; bless His name, bear news of His Salvation (yeshuato) day by day."

98:2-3 (3-4) "YHVH has revealed His Salvation (yeshuato); He unveiled His righteousness to the eyes of the nations. He has remembered His mercy and His faithfulness to the house of Israel; all the ends of the earth have seen the Salvation (Yeshuat) of our God (Elohenu)."

106:4 "Remember me, YHVH, with the favor of Your people; O visit me with Your Salvation (b'yeshuatecha)."

116:13 "I will lift up the cup of Salvation (yeshuot), and I will call on the name of YHVH."

118:14-15 "YHVH is my strength and my song; and He is my Salvation (l'yeshuah)." "The voice of rejoicing and Salvation (v'yeshuah) is in the tabernacle of the righteous; the right hand of YHVH works mightily."

119:123 "My eyes fail for Your Salvation (l'yeshuatecha), and for the word of Your righteousness."

119:155 "Salvation (yeshuah) is far from the wicked; for they do not seek Your statutes."

119:166 "O YHVH, I have hoped for Your Salvation (l'yeshuatecha), and have done Your precepts."

119:174 "I have longed for Your Salvation (l'yeshuatecha), O YHVH; and Your law (torah) is my delight."

140:7 (8)"O YHVH the Lord, the strength of my Salvation (yeshuati), You have covered my head in the day of armor."

149:4 "For YHVH takes pleasure in His people; He adorns the meek with Salvation (b'yeshuah)."

Job (Iyov) 13:16 "He also is my Salvation (l'yeshuah), for an ungodly one shall not come before Him."

I Chronicles (Divrei-HaYamim Alef) 16:23 "Sing to YHVH, all the earth, proclaim His <u>Salvation</u> (yeshuato) from day to day."

II Chronicles (Divrei-HaYamim Bet) 20:17 "You shall not fight in this:station yourselves; stand and see the <u>Salvation</u> (et yeshuat) of YHVH with you, O Judah and Jerusalem; do not be afraid nor fear; tomorrow go out before them, and YHVH shall be with you."

Other verses in the TaNaKH that use a form of the root word יָשַׁע yasha (taken from the Complete Jewish Bible which in the Psalms gives the Hebrew Tanakh verse number first).

Isaiah 45:17 "But Isra'el, saved by ADONAI with an everlasting **salvation,** you will never, ever, be ashamed or disgraced."

Isaiah 46:13 "I am bringing my justice nearer, it is not far away; my **salvation** will not be delayed, I will place my **salvation** in Tziyon for Isra'el my glory."

Jeremiah 3:23b "Truly the **salvation** of Isra'el is in ADONAI our God."

Joel 2:32 "At that time, whoever calls on the name of ADONAI will be **saved**. For in Mount Tziyon and Yerushalayim there will be those who escape, as ADONAI has promised; among the survivors will be those whom ADONAI has called."

Psalms 37:39-40 "ADONAI is the one who **saves** the righteous; he is their stronghold in time of trouble. ADONAI helps them and rescues them, rescues them from the wicked and **saves** them; because they take refuge in him."

Psalm 38:23(22) "Come quickly to help me, Adonai, my **salvation**!"

Psalm 40:11 (10), 17 (16) " 'I did not hide your righteousness in my heart but declared your faithfulness and **salvation**; I did not conceal your grace and truth from the great assembly.' ... But may all those who seek you be glad and take joy in you. May those who love your **salvation** say always, 'ADONAI is great and glorious!' "

Psalm 51:16 (14) "Rescue me from the guilt of shedding blood, God, God of my **salvation**! Then my tongue will sing about your righteousness"

Psalm 71:15 "All day long my mouth will tell of your righteous deeds and acts of **salvation**, though their number is past my knowing."

Psalm 119:41,81 "May your grace come to me, ADONAI, your **salvation**, as you promised. ... I am dying to know your **salvation**; my hope is in your word."

B'rit Hadashah

Gospels

Luke 1:68-69 "Praised be ADONAI, the God of Isra'el, because he has visited and made a ransom to liberate his people by raising up for us a mighty **Deliverer** who is a descendant of his servant David."

Luke 1:76-77 "You, child, will be called a prophet of Ha`Elyon; you will go before the Lord to prepare his way by spreading the knowledge among his people that **deliverance** comes by having sins forgiven."

Luke 2:28-32 "Shim'on took him in his arms, made a b'rakhah to God, and said, 'Now, ADONAI, according to your word, your servant is at peace as you let him go; for I have seen with my own eyes your **yeshu'ah,** which you prepared in the presence of all peoples — a light that will bring revelation to the Goyim and glory to your people Isra'el.' "

Luke 3:4-6 "It was just as had been written in the book of the sayings of the prophet Yesha'yahu, 'The voice of someone crying out: "In the desert prepare the way for ADONAI! Make straight paths for him! Every valley must be filled in, every mountain and hill leveled off; the winding roads must be straightened and the rough ways made smooth. Then all humanity will see God's **deliverance**." ' "

John 4:22-24 "You people don't know what you are worshipping; we worship what we do know, because **salvation** comes from the Jews. But the time is coming — indeed, it's here now — when the true worshippers will worship the Father spiritually and truly, for these are the kind of people the Father wants worshipping him. God is spirit; and worshippers must worship him spiritually and truly."

Acts

Acts 4:11-12 "This Yeshua is the stone rejected by you builders which has become the cornerstone. There is **salvation** in no one else! For there is no other name under heaven given to mankind by whom we must be saved!"

Acts 13:26 "Brothers! — sons of Avraham and those among you who are 'God-fearers'! It is to us that the message of this **deliverance** has been sent!"

Acts 13:47 "For that is what ADONAI has ordered us to do: 'I have set you as a light for the Goyim, to be for **deliverance** to the ends of the earth.' "

Acts 28:28 "Therefore, let it be known to you that this **salvation** of God has been sent to the Goyim, and they will listen!"

Letters of Sha'ul (Paul)

Romans 1:16 "For I am not ashamed of the Good News, since it is God's powerful means of bringing **salvation** to everyone who keeps on trusting, to the Jew especially, but equally to the Gentile."

Romans 10:1-2,10 "Brothers, my heart's deepest desire and my prayer to God for Isra'el is for their **salvation**; for I can testify to their zeal for God. But it is not based on correct understanding; … For with the heart one goes on trusting and thus continues toward righteousness, while with the mouth one keeps on making public acknowledgement and thus continues toward deliverance (Yeshua)."

Romans 11:11-12 " 'In that case, I say, isn't it that they have stumbled with the result that they have permanently fallen away?' Heaven forbid! Quite the contrary, it is by means of their stumbling that the **deliverance** has come to the Gentiles, in order to provoke them to jealousy. Moreover, if their stumbling is bringing riches to the world - that is, if Isra'el's being placed temporarily in a condition less favored than that of the Gentiles is bringing riches to the latter - how much greater riches will Isra'el in its fullness bring them!"

Romans 13:11-12 "Besides all this, you know at what point of history we stand; so it is high time for you to rouse yourselves from sleep; for the final **deliverance** is nearer than when we first came to trust. The night is almost over, the day is almost here. So let us put aside the deeds of darkness and arm ourselves with the weapons of light."

II Corinthians 7:10 "Pain handled in God's way produces a turning from sin to God which leads to **salvation,** and there is nothing to regret in that! But pain handled in the world's way produces only death."

Ephesians 1:13 "Furthermore, you who heard the message of the truth, the Good News offering you **deliverance**, and put your trust in the Messiah were sealed by him with the promised Ruach HaKodesh."

Ephesians 6:17 "And take the helmet of **deliverance** (most versions say 'salvation'); along with the sword given by the Spirit, that is, the Word of God."

II Thessalonians 2:13 "But we have to keep thanking God for you always, brothers whom the Lord loves, because God chose you as first fruits for **deliverance** by giving you the holiness that has its origin in the Spirit and the faithfulness that has its origin in the truth."

II Timothy 3:15-17 "And recalling too how from childhood you have known the Holy Scriptures, which can give you the wisdom that leads to **deliverance** through trusting in Yeshua the Messiah. All Scripture is God-breathed and is valuable for teaching the truth, convicting of sin, correcting faults and training in right living; thus anyone who belongs to God may be fully equipped for every good work."

Titus 2:11 "For God's grace, which brings **deliverance**, has appeared to all people."

Hebrews

Hebrews 2:3 "Then how will we escape if we ignore such a great **deliverance**? This **deliverance**, which was first declared by the Lord, was confirmed to us by those who heard him."

Hebrews 5:9 "And after he had been brought to the goal, he became the source of eternal **deliverance** to all who obey him."

Hebrews 9:27-28 "Just as human beings have to die once, but after this comes judgment, so also the Messiah, having been offered once to bear the sins of many, will appear a second time, not to deal with sin, but to **deliver** those who are eagerly waiting for him."

Letters of Peter

I Peter 1:5,9-10 "Meanwhile, through trusting, you are being protected by God's power for a **deliverance** ready to be revealed at the Last Time. ... And you are receiving what your trust is aiming at, namely, your **deliverance**. The prophets, who prophesied about this gift of **deliverance** that was meant for you, pondered and inquired diligently about it."

The Revelation of Yeshua by Yochanan

Revelation 7:10 "And they shouted, 'Victory (Salvation) to our God, who sits on the throne, and to the Lamb!'"

Revelation 12:10 "Then I heard a loud voice in heaven saying, 'Now have come God's **victory (Salvation),** power and kingship, and the authority of his Messiah; because the Accuser of our brothers, who accuses them day and night before God, has been thrown out!'"

Revelation 19:1 "After these things, I heard what sounded like the roar of a huge crowd in heaven, shouting, 'Halleluyah! The **victory (salvation)**, the glory, the power of our God!' "

Isn't Yeshua wonderful?! I am so full of JOY just reading through these verses! Let's pause for a celebration and sing a song of praise to YHVH for His Salvation

> **"Salvation belongs to our God, who sits on the throne for ever and ever, and to the Lamb who was slain, be glory and power for ever and ever. Amen!"** (From Revelations 7:10,12) [2]

----

[1] Genesis 3:15

[2] Paul Wilbur, "Salvation Belongs to Our God," *Jerusalem Arise* and *Desert Rain* CDs. Also on Youtube at http://www.youtube.com/watch?v=wLdno9i8pyk

14.

Just to Know You, Yeshua

Next I saw heaven opened, and there before me was a white horse. Sitting on it was the one called <u>Faithful and True</u>, and it is in righteousness that he passes judgment and goes to battle. His eyes were like a fiery flame, and on his head were many royal crowns. And <u>he had a name written which no one knew but himself.</u> He was wearing a robe that had been soaked in blood, and the <u>name by which he is called is, "THE WORD OF GOD."</u> The armies of heaven, clothed in fine linen, white and pure, were following him on white horses. And out of his mouth comes a sharp sword with which to strike down nations — "He will rule them with a staff of iron." It is he who treads the winepress from which flows the wine of the furious rage of ADONAI, God of heaven's armies. And on his robe and on his thigh <u>he has a name written: KING OF KINGS AND LORD OF LORDS</u>. (Revelation 19:11-16 CJB)

In response, let us come to appreciate and love the Jewishness of our Messiah Savior—the Lion of the Tribe of Judah. Learn His name and use it! See Him as the scarlet thread throughout the Scriptures as your salvation. See Him in the furnishings of the wilderness Tabernacle (YHVH's dwelling place). Grow to love, honor, and appreciate the Jewish people. Learn about the depths of the Feasts of YHVH and how Yeshua fulfilled them and what can be expected on YHVH's calendar in the future.

It is time to shift from digging to worship. We have found the treasures. It is time to look up and see the bright blue sky and let the warmth of the Light of the "Son" shine in your soul. It is time to respond and let **Him** rebuild and restore. It is time to celebrate.

There is a song I heard and learned several years ago that I sing from time to time. I love the spirit of this song because it is my true cry to Adonai. Here are the words.

Just to Know You [1]

Just to Know You is what I really long for
Just to be with You, You show me who I am
Just to feel Your touch, surrounded by Your Presence
Just to Know You, come and fill me again

Take me deeper in Love with You
To the place I belong
To be held in Your secret place
Where I'm sheltered from the storm
Help me seek not Your hand alone
But to look in Your face
To believe in Your love for me, for there I find release

Just to know You.....

Why don't you take a few moments to reflect and spend some time with Yeshua. If you need to repent, you know that He will hear your prayer and will forgive you. Ask for the veil to be taken off of your eyes. Ask for eyes to see and ears to hear. Ask Yeshua to reveal Himself to you. He has offered a personal relationship. You can hear His voice. He is ready and waiting for you, to wrap you up in a package and send you to the Father, who will rejoice over you with great JOY!

Promised Land

May we come into your presence.
May we bow before your throne.
May we worship you forever.
May you be our only home.

As we're sitting at your table
And we're eating from your hand.
Fill us up so we are able
To possess the promised land.

Hallelujah.
Praise Your Holy Name." [2]

Then I will sprinkle clean water on you, and you will be clean; I will cleanse you from all your uncleanness and from all your idols. I will give you a new heart and put a new spirit inside you; I will take the stony heart out of your flesh and give you a heart of flesh. I will put my Spirit inside you and cause you to live by my laws, respect my rulings and obey them. (Ezekiel 36:25-27)

May I suggest, if you have access to the internet, that you go to http://www.zemerlevav.org/ and listen to their song called "Yeshua." [3] At the bottom of the webpage you will see the title of the song that begins playing. Click on the arrows until "Yeshua - Even There" appears. It will begin to play. Let it be a song of meditation and love for the one who gave it all for you. (The lyrics are on the next page.)

Yeshua [3]

I stand in awe of Your presence
How could You love one such as I?
One humbled sinner.

I stand in awe of Your presence
Why would you die?
For one lost out of the hundred.

Yeshua, Yeshua, Yeshua, Yeshua

I stand in awe of Your wonders
What, Lord, am I?
A drop of dew in a forest.

I stand in awe of Your wonders
What purpose have I?
I live only to Praise You!

Yeshua, Yeshua, Yeshua, Yeshua

You are a shield for me
My Glory and the Lifter of my head.

Baruch Haba B'Shem Adonai
(Blessed is He who comes in the Name of YHVH)

Bo Yeshua, Bo!! (Come Yeshua, Come!!)

----

[1] Wanda Alger, ©2001 *Just To Know You* CD. All rights reserved. Used by permission. http://www.wandaalger.com/index.php?id=15 Also on Amazon.com: http://www.amazon.com/s?ie=UTF8&field-artist=Wanda%20Alger&page=1&rh=n%3A5174%2Cp_32%3AWanda%20Alger.

[2] Words and Music by Rebecca Hazelton, 2011.

[3] Kerah Oliveira, *Even There* CD, © 2011 Zemer Levav.. All rights reserved. Used by permission. http://www.zemerlevav.org/

Appendix A
Prophecies of Messiah in the Tanakh Fulfilled by Yeshua

~~~~~~~

Is it any wonder that the Book in the TaNaKH that has the most prophecies about the Messiah is Yesha'yahu (Isaiah)? He has the same root name as Yeshua!

~~~~~~~~~~~~~~

Yeshua fulfilled hundreds of prophesies in the Scriptures! The odds of one person fulfilling even a few is astronomical! Here is a selection.

Messianic Prophecy

Old Covenant (Torah & Haphtarah)	New Covenant Fulfilled
Messiah's pre-existence.	
Micah 5:2	John 1:1-17
He would come from the seed of a woman.	
Genesis 3:15	Matthew 1:18
	Galatians 4:4
From the seed of Abraham.	
Genesis 12:3	Matthew 1:1-16
From the seed of David.	
Isaiah 11:10	Matthew 1:1
	Acts 13:23
From the tribe of Judah.	
Genesis 49:10	Matthew 1:1-3
	Revelation 5:5
A prophet like Moses.	
Deuteronomy 18:15-19	John 5:45-47
	Acts 3: 20-22
Be preceded by a messenger.	
Malachi 3:1	Luke 1:17
	Matthew 11:7-14

Born of a Virgin.
Isaiah 7:14   Matthew 1:18-21
                               Luke 1:34

Born in Bethlehem.
Micah 5:2   Luke 2:4-2:7
Isaiah 9:6,7   Matthew 2:1

Great persons come to Adore Him.
Psalm 72:10   Matthew 2:1-2,11

He would be poor.
Isaiah 53:2   Luke 9:58
                               Mark 6:3

His ministry in Galilee.
Isaiah 9:1-2   Matthew 4:12,16,23

He would work miracles and healing.
Isaiah 35:5-6; 61:1-2   Matthew 11:4-6
                               Luke 4:16-21
                               John 9:25-38

He Enters Jerusalem humbly on a donkey.
Zechariah 9:9   Matthew 21:1-9

He is Hated without a cause.
Psalm 69:4   John 15:24-25
Isaiah 49:7

Jews and Gentiles both come against Him.
Psalm 2:1-2   Acts 4:25-28

He is sold for 30 pieces of silver.
Zechariah 11:12-13   Matthew 26:15; 27:3,7

His disciples forsake Him.
Zechariah 11:12   Matthew 26:56

He is rejected, tried, condemned, wounded, pierced, and is silent before His accusers .
Isaiah 53   Matthew 27
Psalm 22; 69:8   Mark 14
Zechariah 12:10   Luke 23
                               John 1:11,19

No bones would be broken.
Psalm 34:20   John 19:33
He would intercede for his murderers.
Isaiah 53:12   Luke 23:24
He would be buried in a rich man's tomb.
Isaiah 53:9   Matthew 27:57-60
Die for the sins of Israel & the World
  and bring Salvation.
Isaiah 25:9-10; 53:5-6   Matthew 20:28
                          Luke 19:9-10
                          John 3:14-21
Messiah must die before the 2nd Temple
  is destroyed.
Daniel 9:24-27 Temple destroyed in 70 AD
Yeshua died between 30-33 AD
He would rise from the dead.
Psalm 16:10   Matthew 28
Isaiah 53:10   Mark 16
                          Luke 24
                          John 20
He would ascend into heaven.
Psalm 68:18   Luke 24:51
He is sitting at the right hand of Elohim.
Psalm 110:1   Hebrews 1:3
He would be a Light to the Gentiles (Goyim).
Isaiah 11:10; 42:1-7   Luke 2:25-32
Isaiah 49:1-8   Acts 10:45
His message would be spread world-wide.
Isaiah 49:6;56:8   Matthew 24:14; 28:19
Amos 9:12   Acts 15:15-18
He will come again in judgment and kingship.
Psalm 24:7-10   Matthew 24
Daniel 7:13-14   Revelation 1:7,19
Numbers 24:14,17-19

	Appendix B : HOLIDAYS COMMONLY OBSERVED BY THE CHURCH		
Holiday	Pagan / Occult Origin	Pagan/Occult Practices	"Christian" Context
Lent	Weeping for Tammuz, son of god Nimrod (Tower of Babel fame) and goddess Semiramis. (see Ezekiel 8:14)	Ashes 40 days for 40 years of Tammuz	Temptation of Jesus – 40 days in wilderness fasting. 40 days before Easter. Pope decreed in 519 CE
Palm Sunday	N/A – timed with Easter		Jesus' entry into Jerusalem
Maundy Thursday	N/A – timed with Easter		Lord's Supper – Really is the Passover Seder
Good Friday	N/A – timed with Easter		Jesus' Crucifixion – If Yeshua was to be three days and nights in the "belly of the earth" then this day is incorrect.
Easter Sunday	Fertility Rites of Spring Name of the Goddess Isis/ Ashteroth/Oster – and others – the Queen of Heaven. (See Jeremiah 7:16-18; 42-44, especially 44:15-30 and Ezekiel 8)	Easter Bunny, Colored Eggs, Easter bonnets, Easter Basket, New Dresses, Sunrise observances, Eating Ham (because Tammuz's death was by a "boar" who "bored" him)	Resurrection of Jesus

Appendix B : HOLIDAYS COMMONLY OBSERVED BY THE CHURCH (cont.)			
Holiday	Pagan / Occult Origin	Pagan/Occult Practices	"Christian" Context
Christmas	Birth of Mithra –Sun God, also known by other names. Winter Solstice rites. Day of Saturalia – head of all gods. Yule – Chaldea name for infant/child Arabian worship – Birthday of the lord, the moon (Meni) – see Is.65:11)	Mistletoe, Christmas wreath, Holly, Santa Claus, Reindeer, giving of presents, Christmas tree	Birth of Jesus – There is no biblical basis for the date of the birth of Yeshua. Technically, it could not have been in winter based on Scriptures regarding the shepherds. Also, the wise men were not at the manger as commonly depicted in Nativity scenes and plays.

(Cont.)

Other Holidays with Pagan/Occult origins commonly observed by church members

Holiday	Pagan / Occult Origin	Pagan/Occult Practices	
Valentine's Day	Fertility rite of Cupid, son of Venus, daughter of Jupiter a fertility goddess.	Sweets, flowers, human heart.	It's important to be careful what you are celebrating on this holiday.
Groundhog Day	Divine future – maiden , mother, crone cycle. Earth goddess sleeps inside the earth in winter	Represented by a groundhog and tied in with timing before Spring Equinox festivals.	Mostly this holiday is foolishness and an excuse for men to get drunk and have a party.
May Day	High holy day of earth religions. Beltain Fertility rites	May pole – Fallic symbol, dancing/intertwining of ribbons signifies fertility rite – unification of sexual organs	Don't be fooled by the supposed "innocence" of these "rites" of spring.
St. Patrick's Day	Sacrifice of children for financial blessings and good luck	Leprochans and shalalies are tools of the god to lure the children.	Be aware of "opening" a door for the adversary.
Halloween	Highest holy day of earth religions and satan worshipers. Sanhain.	Fire festival. Stone circles, human sacrifice, giant cauldron, bobbing for apples, trick or treat, carved pumpkins to keep evil spirits away, costumes and masks	If anyone is celebrating this holiday or masking it with a Harvest Festival, they need to really search out the scriptures for the truth. This is the most evil of all the holidays and must be avoided at all costs.

Recommended Reading

Appel, Rabbi Jim, *Yom Teruah: The Day of Sounding the Shofar* – Appointed Times Series, Olive Press Christian and Messianic Publisher, Copenhagen, NY, 2011.

Brown, Michael L., *Answering Jewish Objections to Jesus*, Volumes 1-5, Baker Books, Grand Rapids, MI, 2007.

Cantor, Ron, *Identity Theft: One Jewish Man's Search For Truth And The Battle To Keep Him From Finding It*, Destiny Image Publishers, Inc, Shippensburg, PA, 2013.

Doron, Reuven, *One New Man*, Embrace Israel Ministries, Cedar Rapids, IA, 2003.

Finto, Don, *Your People Shall Be My People: How Israel, The Jews And The Christian Church Will Come Together In The Last Days*, Regal Books, Gospel Light, Ventura, CA, 2001.

Garr, John D., *Our Lost Legacy*, Golden Keys Press, 2006.

Gordon, Nehemia, *The Hebrew Yeshua vs. the Greek Jesus: New Light on the Seat of Moses from Shem-Tov's Hebrew Matthew*, Hilkiah Press (www.hilkiahpress.com), 2005.

Hershberg, Rabbi Greg, *From the Projects to the Palace*, Olive Press Messianic and Christian Publisher, Copenhagen, NY, 2012.

Hislop, Rev. Alexander, *The Two Babylons*, Presbyterian Free Church of Scotland, 1919, – an old English volume – quite tedious but well worth the effort. Can be found on line at: http://www.biblebelievers.com/babylon/00index.htm.

Juster, Dan, *Jewish Roots, A Foundation of Biblical Theology*, Destiny Image Publishers, Inc., Shippensburg, PA, 1986, Third edition 1995.

Katz, Art, *Israel and the Church in Psalm 102,* audio message found at http://artkatzministries.org/audio-messages/k-312-israel-and-the-church-in-psalm-102/.

Moseley, Dr. Ron, *Yeshua, A Guide to the Real Jesus and the Original Church,* Messianic Jewish Publishers, Clarksville, MD, 1998.

Pritz, Roy A., *Nazarene Jewish Christianity,* The Hebrew University Magnes Press, Jerusalem, Israel, 1988.

Roth, Andrew Gabriel, *Aramaic English New Testament,* Fifth Edition, Netzari Press LLC, 2012. A compilation, annotation, and translation of the Eastern Original Aramaic New Testament Pashitta Text. The Aramaic is featured with Hebrew letters and vowel pointings.

Sampson, Robin, *A Family Guide to Biblical Holidays,* – an excellent guide to observing Biblical Holidays with ideas for children and how to teach them. Heart of Wisdom Publishing, www.heartofwisdom.org, 2001

Schneider, Joy A., *Identifying the Hierarchy of Satan: A Handbook for Wrestling to Win!* Water of Life Unlimited, Fort Colins, Co, 2002.

Stern, David A., *Restoring the Jewishness of the Gospel,* Jewish New Testament Publisher, Clarkesville, MD, 1988, 1990, 2009.

Stern, David H., *Complete Jewish Bible* and *Jewish New Testament Commentary,* Jewish New Testament Publications, Inc. Clarksville, MD, 1992.

Tozer, A.W., *Divine Conquest,* published in Mass Market Press by Living Books, 1995. – Mr. Tozer lived from 1897 – 1963 and wrote prolifically, challenging the Christian church in many areas.

For His Name YESHUA

is available at:
olivepresspublisher.com
amazon.com
barnesandnoble.com
and other online stores

Store managers:
Order wholesale through
Ingram Book Company
or by emailing:
olivepressbooks@gmail.com

City of David, excavation site

CPSIA information can be obtained at www.ICGtesting.com
Printed in the USA
LVOW04s0907070915

452608LV00034B/148/P